The Magic Glass

By the same author

Renaissance Spain in its Literary Relations with England and France: A Critical Bibliography

THE

MAGIC GLASS

The Individual and Society As Seen in
the Gams of Herman Melville's *Moby-Dick*

Hilda Urén Stubbings

Rubena Press
Bloomington, Indiana

1992

The text of this book was written in *Nota Bene* and typeset in Adobe Palatino using *Ventura Publisher*. Book design by R. G. Stubbings. Bound by Franklin 's Bindery, Spencer, Indiana.

First published 1992

Cataloging-in-Publication Data
            Stubbings, Hilda Urén
                The Magic Glass
                Bibliography, p.   Includes index.
                    1. Melville, Herman, 1819-1891—Moby-Dick. 2.
                Fiction—19th century—Criticism and interpreta-
                tion. 3. United States in literature. I. Title.
    PS2384 M62 .S8   813'.3
    ISBN 1-880622-00-9   Library of Congress Catalog Card Number 91-67127

Rubena Press, 2500 East Eighth Street, Bloomington IN 47408-4215

The paper used in this publication meets the minimum requirements of the American National Standard for Information Sciences—Permanence of Paper for Printed Library Materials, ANSI Z39.48-1984

To George, who patiently (or impatiently) read the many drafts, because he felt that these ideas should be shared with other lovers of literature.

To Robert, whose enthusiasm got the project started and whose computer-expertise made the publication possible.

"Close! stand close to me, Starbuck; let me look into a human eye; it is better than to gaze upon God. By the green land; by the bright hearthstone! this is the magic glass. . . ."—From *Moby-Dick*, Ahab's words in "The Symphony."

And some certain significance lurks in all things, else all things are little worth, and the round world itself but an empty cipher.—From *Moby-Dick*, "The Doubloon."

Table of Contents

Preface

This monograph presupposes somewhat more than a nodding acquaintance with Herman Melville's classic work, *Moby-Dick*, for it deals with specific parts of the novel, namely, what Melville calls the "gams." These mini-dramas, nine in number, are interspersed throughout the narrative whenever the *Pequod* encounters another whaling vessel, either outward or homeward bound. Therefore it is hoped that the reader will have with him or her a copy of *Moby-Dick* as a trusty companion, or *vade mecum*, to make this monograph more intelligible and therefore more enjoyable. Throughout the work I have referred to many parts of the novel which relate to the themes of the gams with the hope that this will encourage readers to delve even more deeply into Melville's own writings.

Melville satisfies our curiosity regarding just what a gam is in the parlance of whaling men:

> Gam. Noun—A social meeting of two (or more) Whale Ships, generally on a cruising-ground; when, after exchanging hails, they exchange visits by boats' crews; the two captains remaining, for the time, on board of one ship, and the two chief mates on the other....

Gamming is an intensely social custom, necessitated by the long periods of time—up to four years—that whalers spent on the ocean. Whaling men were a breed of their own, and only their comrades could understand them. Therefore these gams were looked forward to with great enthusiasm. In *Moby-Dick*, however, Ahab deprived his crew of the jollity they had a right to expect because, as they find out after the voyage has begun, they have contracted their souls to Captain Ahab's macabre enterprise, the entrapping and killing of a certain mysterious White Whale which has become an all-consuming fetish. Instead of a friendly greeting when another whaler approaches, "Have ye seen the White Whale?" has become for the look-outs of the *Pequod* a shibboleth which, according to Ahab's orders, must immediately follow the customary hearty "Ship ahoy!" The gam which ensues depends for its character upon the answer to that question.

On the vast expanses of ocean are met the *Albatross*, the *Town-Ho*, the *Jeroboam*, the *Virgin* (or *Jungfrau*), the *Rose Bud* (or *Bouton de Rose*), the *Samuel Enderby of London*, the *Bachelor*, the *Rachel*, and the *Delight*. Melville has made each gam unique: each one serves as a mirror of human relationships, on board the *Pequod* and in its interactions with sister-ships.

As the title suggests, the structure of this monograph is two-fold: first the gams are introduced more specifically as reflections of interrelationships of persons; following that they are treated as representations of wider themes which mirror Melville's oft-expressed attitudes toward his society as it rushed headlong into an industrialization which, he believed, was inimical to humane values, paralleling Ahab's rush to steer the *Pequod* toward its calamitous encounter with Moby Dick.

In the end the vision which Ahab has seen in the "magic glass" of Starbuck's gaze leads him to a last effort to recapture a portion of his humaneness by an order to Starbuck to remain on the *Pequod* during the fatal chase. This effort is frustrated, however, when the final disaster becomes too overwhelming even for Ahab to control. Moby Dick becomes the final arbiter of Fate.

The idea for this inquiry came in the course of an inspiring Charles E. Merrill American Studies seminar conducted by Dr. John A. Hague, Professor and Chair of the Department of American Studies at Stetson University, and Dr. Albert E. Stone, Jr., then of Emory University, and later of the University of Iowa. The idea subsequently developed into a subject for a master's thesis in American Studies; the present work has suffered through many drafts before it seemed to be in a publishable form, so rich is the subject matter.

Since that time Herman Melville's work has lost none of its relevance and continues to be the subject of many courses and seminars all over the nation. In foreign countries Melville is admired and read and has become the focus of much critical attention—in fact, it was in Britain that the Melvillian renaissance first took shape in the 1920's. In France such a discerning critic as the existentialist writer Albert Camus joined the growing ranks of Melville's enthusiasts. This phenomenon is due to the fact that Melville's ideas and metaphors are probably more appreciated by readers and critics of the twentieth century than those of the nineteenth, when he was generally misunderstood.

Although whaling is no longer an acceptable enterprise, this does not deter the increasing number of fascinated Melville readers who find in *Moby-Dick* testimony to some of the most valued American attributes: love of Nature, daring, resourcefulness, and comradeship. It is hoped that these readers will find echoes of their fascination in this little book.

Writers always incur a great number of debts along the way as a manuscript turns into a book. Here I will gladly acknowledge some of them: to Susi, Caye, Bob, and Carl—I well remember how we all worked together that summer in Florida to make the thesis come to life; to Sue Kaman for taking time out of her busy days to read the revised manuscript and make many helpful, incisive comments; to Norm Rosenthal for his consistent concern, and, not at all least, to my students who took to heart the perennial question "What is an American?"—and provided me with heartening answers. Moreover, "top-gallant" thanks to Dr. John A. Hague, who was kind enough to read the proofs and whose critical suggestions helped keep me on a even keel in sometimes treacherous waters.

Writers, too, usually claim for themselves and themselves alone blame for any and all mistakes which may be found, and I follow their laudable example with a willing *mea culpa*.

Finally, gratitude to the late Dr. Gerald E. Wade of Vanderbilt University, without whose encouragement I might not have set sail on this voyage at all.

H. U. S.

Bloomington, Indiana

Cast of Characters

Captain Ahab. Captain of the *Pequod*, a whaler from Nantucket. He is maimed, having lost a leg to the White Whale, Moby Dick. Ahab has a family in Nantucket.

Starbuck. Captain Ahab's first mate. Starbuck has a family in Nantucket.

Stubb. Captain Ahab's second mate, a native of Cape Cod.

Flask. Captain Ahab's third mate, a native of Martha's Vineyard.

Ishmael. Known as the "wanderer," he is the seaman on the *Pequod* who chronicles the voyage. He is also seen as Melville's *persona*.

Queequeq. One of the *Pequod's* harpooneers, a native of Kokovoko (possibly in the Figi Islands). He was Ishmael's first friend amongst the crew.

Daggoo. A Negro from Africa, one of the harpooneers on the *Pequod*.

Tashtego. An American Indian from north Martha's Vineyard, one of the harpooneers of the *Pequod*.

Radney. First mate and part owner on the *Town-Ho* and Steelkilt's enemy. Radney was from Martha's Vineyard.

Steelkilt. Sailor and leader of a mutiny on the *Town-Ho* and Radney's enemy. Steelkilt was from Buffalo.

Don Sebastian and *Don Pedro*. Two of Ishmael's aristocratic South American friends whom he visited in the Golden Inn in Lima, Peru.

Captain Mayhew. Captain of the *Jeroboam*, a whaler from Nantucket, which has an epidemic on board.

Gabriel. Fanatical leader of a mutiny on the *Jeroboam*.

Captain Derick De Deer. Captain of the German whaler, the *Jungfrau* (or *Virgin*), which had run out of oil.

Captain of the French whaler, the *Bouton de Rose* (or *Rose Bud*), which carries "blasted" whales.

Guernsey man. First mate and interpreter on the *Bouton de Rose*.

Captain Boomer. Captain of the *Samuel Enderby of London.* He also is maimed, having lost an arm to Moby Dick.

Dr. Bunger. Ship's surgeon on the *Samuel Enderby*.

Captain Gardiner. Captain of a whaler from Nantucket, the *Rachel*, which rescues Ishmael while searching for lost crewmen.

Also captains of the whalers *Albatross, Town-Ho, Bachelor,* and *Delight* (all of Nantucket).

1

Introduction

The search for symbols in literature and their interpretation afford rich opportunities for the discovery of parallels and varied levels of meaning which stimulate the creative reader and literary critic. The quest for meaning is basic to all artistic creation. Often the artist finds that his or her intuition of truth can be conveyed only by symbols or by dramatizations which suggest instead of delineating. This method invites many interpretations. The role of criticism is to add its perception to that of the author and thus elucidate, happily, what the author has to say.

Stormy controversy concerning the symbolic character of Herman Melville's writings has often swirled around *Moby-Dick*, with the literalists declaring stoutly that it is nothing more than a good sea adventure story. This attitude has some validity, for hardly a critic can doubt Melville's expertise in cetology. Moreover, it is apparent that his interest in whaling was genuine, being based on his years as a seafarer, and therefore it was not just a suitable conveyance for his philosophy or to be used as an allegorical reference. Other readers of a more poetic or philosophic frame of mind would consider the whaling structure secondary. It is quite obvious that Melville himself wished to stir in his readers interpretations other than the literal one, for his work is rich in allegorical allusions and philosophical digressions. Moreover, the experiences gleaned from his voyages provided him with metaphors for life on many levels and gave him deep insights into human motivations.

The many-faceted genius of Melville's intuitive knowledge is graphically displayed in *Moby-Dick*. Adaptable to so many fertile interpretations, this book's symbolisms or parallels can sustain several levels of meaning, from the most literal and simple to the most mystical and complex. As Charles Feidelson, Jr., comments, "No interpretation is adequate that fails to take into account the multiplicity of possible meanings in the White Whale and in *Moby-Dick* as a whole." The White Whale can be all things to all men, from the representation of ultimate reality to the embodiment of a personal goal, with Ahab a cultural hero, a seeker after knowledge, Everyman or merely an obsessed mariner on a quest for personal revenge.[1] Another critic wrote in defense of the symbolic interpretation of Melville's writings:

> Melville gives hints . . . that his mind at times moved to a plane where he saw things in a way we will call phantasmal, because our intelligence cannot do it. What he knew cannot be related to anything we know. . . .[2]

---

[1] See Feidelson's introduction to his edition of *Moby-Dick* (Indianapolis: Bobbs-Merrill Company, 1964) for several interpretations. This edition is very useful for its copious annotations, maps, and illustrations.

[2] Anonymous, "The Vogue of Herman Melville," in the British journal, *The Nation & The Athenaeum*, for September 30, 1922. This reference is included in *Moby-Dick as Doubloon: Essays and Extracts, 1851-1970*, edited by Hershel Parker and Harrison Hayford (New York: W. W. Norton, 1970).

If this novel were to be approached as simply a whaling story, the twentieth century would place little except historical value on it, since the hunting of whales has become an offensive, even a criminal, pursuit.[3] But in Melville's youth, whales were looked upon as an inexhaustible resource whose varied uses were indispensable to society, not only for everyday necessities but even, as Melville says, ". . .to light the gay bridals and other merrymakings of men. . . ." The whalemen who risked their lives to procure these essentials were to be admired (if society at large noticed them at all) for their courage, skill, and stoicism—all of which were imperative to have an even chance of coming back from the grueling whale cruises alive. Perhaps the chances of coming back were not even: in *Extracts* Melville enters the note: "It is generally well known that out of the crews of Whaling vessels (American) few ever return in the ships on board of which they departed."[4] Melville himself did a four-year stint on a whaling vessel, and he knew well the risks run by the intrepid men, such as those described in the gam of the *Virgin* (or *Jungfrau*), in "The First Lowering," as well as in the three chapters which describe the final chase for Moby Dick. At that time whales were often looked upon as "killers"— plentiful ones at that—and Melville's White Whale, Moby Dick, has been seen as a symbol of malevolence. Too, Melville had learned from experience how realistic was the picture in Thomas

---

[3] Compare Richard H. Dana, Jr.'s *Two Years before the Mast*, which has been deservedly praised for its detailed portrayal of life on sailing ships but is neglected now. Melville was intrigued by it and wrote to Dana.

[4] Death was not the only cause—mutiny was not uncommon and many, like Melville himself, jumped ship to get away from intolerable conditions.

Beale's *History of the Sperm Whale* (1839), which he quotes in *Extracts*:

> Mad with the agonies he endures from these fresh attacks, the infuriated Sperm Whale rolls over and over; he rears his enormous head, and with wide expanded jaws snaps at everything around him; he rushes at the boats with his head; they are propelled before him with vast swiftness, and sometimes utterly destroyed.

Although the business of whaling has rightfully fallen into disrepute, *Moby-Dick* as an allegory of human life is valued as one of the masterpieces of American literature. In this novel Melville has created for us a kind of artifact, a memorial, which will continue to be read by every serious student of American literature and cultural history. It is a story of fury and revenge which illustrates, as Melville might well say, the Biblical admonition: "Vengeance is mine, saith the Lord—I will repay." Yet underlying this harsh theme there are undertones of compassion which, though not so obvious, are consistent. Moreover, there are many passages which illustrate unmistakably the psychology of the men who are, in essence, reflections of their society and of human nature in general.

It is not my intention to treat Ahab as universal Man sailing upon the ocean as the Cosmos in which Moby Dick represents a chimerical cosmic principle. This has been competently done by a myriad of devoted critics. I view him, at least in part, as representative of human beings who, because they have power granted by society, endeavor to usurp the thoughts and volition of others for a vainglorious undertaking. Because of the spiritual passivity of the members of Ahab's crew and his magnetic personality—the charisma which derives its force from his obsession—Ahab succeeds in this usurpation with one exception: Starbuck.

Starbuck is the rational yet compassionate man who sees no reason for killing for the sake of killing, for the exploitation of Nature for useless purposes. Ahab gives him grudging respect, yet sees him as an impediment to the success of his obsessive quest, for Starbuck's priorities lie elsewhere—with his wife and child back in Nantucket. For Ahab Starbuck is also an uncomfortable reminder of his past: Starbuck's eye is the "magic glass" in which Ahab guiltily sees the reflection of what he was and what he now forcefully rejects. Yet Ahab gleefully congratulates himself because he is well aware that Starbuck is caught in a conflict of values which cluster around the tenets of morality. This is the test of what Melville calls "valor."

The meaning of the gams resides principally in the spirit of the crew of the *Pequod*, where we see their varying attitudes toward social relationships. Because of Melville's emphasis upon the responsibility of the individual, the gams take on added significance in the novel. It is through these seemingly peripheral segments of the novel that we see the men who share the dangerous enterprise of whaling, and we learn of the comparative extent of their "valor" through their thoughts and actions. In opposition to Ahab, they succeed in retaining their humanity and their sanity (Fedallah and Pip aside). After the last chance of human contact has been negated by Ahab when he rudely rebuffed the *Rachel*, we learn from the graphic description of the last and fatal chase that all that was "human, reasonable, and sane" had not been lost by the crew. They hold onto their humanity, which even includes humor and buffoonery, in spite of all the stresses and deprivations of their voyage with the hallucinatory Ahab. Starbuck thinks of his wife and child back in Nantucket, for whose welfare he has made this calamitous pact with Ahab; Flask thinks of his mother, who will be penniless without his wages after he drowns. Moreover, most of the men, especially Starbuck, are solicitous about Ahab and do what they can to ease his physical pain and mental distress when his boat is capsized twice. Tashtego, the "heathen" harpooneer, shows his fierce loyalty to Ahab by continuing his furious hammerings to secure the ship's flag to the mainmast as he disappears with the *Pequod* into the sea. Stubb, the pragmatist, indulges in some self-pity, as well as some defiance and resignation.

These simple responses at the moment of death attest to the validity of Melville's symbol of the return of the *Rachel*— they affirm the strength of human kinship. This makes the voyage-long desolation of the gams even more tragic: in his selfishness Ahab deprives his crew of the fundamental emotional needs which they, unlike him, have never renounced. It is Ahab who has eschewed all that is human.

Says Melville in "The Doubloon," "And some certain significance lurks in all things, else all things are little worth, and the round world itself but an empty cipher. . . ." From this we must believe that the gams have multi-level, often opaque messages. It is for us, the readers, to consider what they are. Therefore these present interpretations are offered as a contribution to the ever-broadening appreciation of the richness of *Moby-Dick*.

In the following pages the gams may be seen as mirrors within which are imaged some of Melville's insights into human existence. His thought often centered upon the possibility of an intuitive knowledge of the nature of reality. Much of what he believed to be true has been confirmed by twentieth-century findings in the fields of psychology and sociology, truths which, as Melville well knew, were often embedded in traditional religious writings. Though he had broken away from the strict Calvinism of his youth, the concepts preached so hardily by its devotees made an indelible impression upon him. He thought of the pursuit after truth in constructive ways, in spite of the fact that he seemed to his generation to be an iconoclast. Instead of wishing to destroy every icon, he intended to coalesce what he saw as enduring truths of civilization with his own insights. It was inevitable that he would be misunderstood. For many reasons Melville had to wait for the twentieth century to be wholly accepted, reasons rooted in part in the fact that his work was anticipatory. One critic would say he had the gift of prophecy; another that he could see more clearly than his contemporaries, who were blinded by the emotions and events of the times—that the things he saw and wrote about were there for all to see, but only a Melville would allow himself to see them.

Viewed from another perspective, one can see that the world changed. A different psychological state made people more amenable to the ideas which Melville had tried to communicate: in other words, the Western world finally caught up to Melville. Much of this was due to the psychological dislocations caused by World War I.[5] Many cherished ideals were rejected after the greatest carnage the world had ever

---

[5] H. M. Tomlinson notes the changes in attitudes following World War I which led to a new appreciation of Melville. See his *Gifts of Fortune* (London: William Heinemann, 1926). Excerpted in Parker and Hayford, 169f.

known seemed to have been all in vain, for world peace was certainly not achieved. Religious beliefs were questioned, faith in governments was undermined, the secure moorings which people had always trusted seemed to have become less secure. It is not surprising that the Melville renaissance began among critics in Britain in the 1920's.[6] Too, the era of the 1930's became another time of questioning: it was an age of "debunking," when the reputations of heretofore heroes were subjected to not always kindly scrutiny. Moreover, even in the field of science new discoveries were causing doubt as to the veracity of usual explanations concerning the universe, and the Freudian revolution called into question the nature of man. Melville gained in prestige as his open-mindedness became more acceptable, as did his candor concerning the underpinnings of society: church, state, national goals, industry, the pursuit of money, and other hitherto sacrosanct human enterprises. Since that time interest in Melville's work has not flagged.

Moby-Dick was the catalyst which led readers to discover the *corpus* of Melville's work. Accent upon the tragic themes within it became the preoccupation of the critics, and the symbolisms fascinated the more romantic. Ahab was the figure which drew the most attention, for he is the most compelling character, the one easiest to point to as carrying the interpretation of Melville's meaning. Ahab's concern with the White Whale and his own cosmic place seemed to leave no leeway for his relationships with anyone else.

---

[6] This is not to say that other nations did not suffer from the war, but Melville was more accessible to the British, being part of the English-speaking tradition.

Melville's concentration upon human relationships may not seem conspicuous in *Moby-Dick*, but one cannot deny the existence of the gams in the novel, and, if his own word is to be trusted, Melville created nothing without meaning. Upon close examination the gams of *Moby-Dick* appear to be illustrations of varying kinds of human relationships which are skilfully portrayed to carry messages which extend past Ahab's characterization. By showing the frustrations of human relationships as they too often occur and by carrying the story of the ill-fated *Pequod* to the disaster which is the logical consequence of Ahab's obsession, Melville implies that we should turn the coin (a doubloon) and reason that, since Ahab's way could lead only to calamity, perhaps another way—obeying God by "disobeying ourselves" (implying our primitive being, the unredeemed self) in each social exchange as Father Mapple urged—might bring us to a different conclusion. Even so, no outcome can be completely free of paradox.[7] *Moby-Dick* is replete with paradoxes, some of which appear in the spiritual "circumnavigation" heralded by the gam of the *Albatross* and finally rounded out by the reappearance of the *Rachel*.

Ahab's characterization is not the only mirror of flawed relationships. Stubb, who is a hearty, likeable fellow, is shown in the gams of the *Jungfrau* and the *Bouton de Rose* with all his socially-approved faults, one of them greed. Yet, to show the limitless intricacy of human nature, it is Stubb who first shows compassion on the captain of the *Rachel*—"What

---

[7] See Father Mapple's exhortations in Chapter IX, "The Sermon."

says Ahab? We must save that boy!" he exclaims. Starbuck, on the other hand, has been compared to a wavering Hamlet in his inability to confront Ahab when he feels that he is heading them all to disaster, but this is not the whole truth, either, for Starbuck combines compassion with great physical bravery as is shown in the gam of the *Jungfrau* and elsewhere.[8] Each man of the crew brings to the ship's community his own individuality and is judged by his crewmates and by the reader accordingly. *Moby-Dick* is essentially the story of Captain Ahab and his vengeful quest for the White Whale. The gams, those social dramas, are stories that belong to the crew.

Only Ishmael, the enigmatic chronicler, survives the ordeal of the *Pequod*. Though every gam has its element of nihilism, the final outcome reaffirms the permanence of human kinship as the men assist each other in the fatal chase. Yet even this reaffirmation is not a ringing victory. Because Ishmael has lost good friends, especially the companionable Queequeg, he must begin his own circumnavigation again—and Melville from the outset has told us that "round the world" is a futile, meaningless concept. After his rescue Ishmael is quite likely to be in the same frame of mind as in the first chapter of the book, where he tells us that whenever he is in a black depression, he goes to sea—and this is just what he did again.

By so tellingly depicting the men of the *Pequod* as they endure the rigors of their "preordained," lonely voyage, Melville has created a testament to courage and comrade-

---

[8] Starbuck's soliloquy, comparable to Hamlet's, is found in "The Musket."

ship. These mariners of the mystical *Pequod* have confronted Fate together, reasonably or recklessly, and together they have disappeared—only to gain immortality on the pages of *Moby-Dick*.

Through his intense involvement with the fate of his characters Melville communicates to his readers his conviction that human existence has no cosmic meaning that we can ever discover, yet most human beings demand meaning, not realizing that the meaning is to be found in the experience itself, the relationships with those who share our quest. This constitutes the essence, and the paradox, of the quest.

Unless we accept without demur the tenets of a religion or other mode of systematic thought we shall have no definite answers. For the majority of Melville's contemporaries, the traditional *ethos* held answers enough—with certain adjustments and elaborations. In spite of his religious upbringing, Melville was not satisfied with derivative values but sought those he could corroborate by his own experience or intuition. It appears that in this context the precepts of mid-century Christianity as they were observed—or "honored in the breach"—were increasingly disturbing to him: Christianity seemed to embody the principles by which human happiness would finally be attained, but it could not succeed unless some way could be found to reconcile its teachings with the positive values of other cultures as well. Although Melville often used Biblical references, his essential philosophy—the ideals by which future generations would live in harmony, he believed—seems more attuned to the New Testament, the seminal book of Christian teachings, than to the Old, yet he found much relevance in *Ecclesiastes* and *Job*.

The quest for Melville was the search for truth—and he hoped to take his readers with him on this quest.[9] Reality, he implies, consists in sharing the perils of the uncharted sea of the Cosmos with one's fellow human beings. Without that sharing, the voyage becomes one of chasing after a "phantom demon," as Ahab's had. Thus the illustrative value of the gams is obvious: in them we see how pridefully Ahab rejects the substance of life, kinship with others. We could say that he realized too late that he was wrong, but this, too, is uncertain. Melville shows him at times almost regretful of his isolation and his hard-heartedness, but at the last we know that he would not or could not have done otherwise—as Ahab himself said, he was fated to do what he did.[10] In the end, with the sinking of the *Pequod* and his own approaching death, Ahab realizes that Moby Dick has won, but he boastfully declares that he has reached the zenith of his greatness (even though he also admits that he is grieving for having failed) without thinking of the men who had lost their lives. That he is willing to sacrifice himself to that endeavor is his prerogative as a free man, but his offense is that he would uncaringly sacrifice others as well.[11]

Melville seems convinced that the way to the solution of humanity's problems lies in increasing our communication

---

[9] "Like the story it tells, our reading of this book is a kind of quest," observes Feidelson, p. xxv.

[10] Throughout *Mardi* Melville emphasizes the paradoxes inherent in the quests humans embark upon, only to come to realize that there are no absolutes to be grasped.

[11] We may call Ahab a free man, but he himself often questioned whether he had free will.

with each other by a relinquishing of the demands of the imperious ego, a forgetting of the self in true regard for others. "Disobeying ourselves," is the hardest thing we shall ever have to do. According to realists, this probably will never be achieved, harried and entrapped as most humans are by inexorable natural forces and the civilization which they themselves have created, one which becomes more relentless as the demands and seductions of the machine age threaten to make automata out of living people.[12]

The effects of the mechanization of human activities, with its concomitant, the trivialization of human emotions, formed a source of themes in Melville's writings. He could not accept the prevalent idea that process should replace spontaneity. The young women workers in "The Tartarus of Maids" illustrate this dichotomy, which in its most extreme form could constitute a polarization of life and death.

In the twentieth century the extreme limit of this mechanization, this sacrifice of all to science, with its devotion to process (specifically scientific method), was embodied in the creation of nuclear weapons. The fact that scientists and engineers gave mankind the means to destroy civilization endued them even more surely with a patina of ultimate power. Yet the luster which they had thereby gained was dimmed when the reality of their Faustian actions dawned upon them.

A disillusioned Albert Einstein, regretting the aftermath of science and technology's crowning achievement, the atomic bomb, exclaimed in 1945:

---

[12]Illustrative of this is Melville's short story, "Bartleby the Scrivener," written to emphasize this alienation and the revolt against it.

I believe that the horrifying deterioration in the ethical conduct of people today stems from the mechanization and dehumanization of our lives. The disastrous by-product of the development of the scientific and technical mentality is guilty. Man grows cold faster than the planets in the heavens. . . . Spirit must overcome technology.

"Spirit must overcome technology." Melville had said this, too, a hundred years before. His prophecies had come true: it appeared that people had indeed become more or less willing slaves to technology's marvels.

This is not what Melville had anticipated: that the encroachment of materialism and technology would be welcomed by the people for whom he wished to be a spokesman. The personal and social progress he envisioned was of another kind, one which would have greater spiritual dimensions, one which would enhance, not diminish, the highest qualities of the human spirit. Yet he was a realist, too: the actions of the characters in the gams are not romanticized: these men speak for themselves.

The gams of *Moby-Dick* show much of what Melville thought of the civilization of his time; as it appeared to him, it seems, it was a frail ship carrying frail human beings on a voyage across the known seas—which seas were, at the same time, far beyond human power of understanding. In these gams, then, are messages we may find relevant for our own century.

2

What Is a Gam?[1]

"Look at the godly, honest, unostentatious, hospitable, social, free-and easy-whaler! What does the whaler do when she meets another whaler in any sort of decent weather? She has a *Gam*, a thing so utterly unknown to all other ships that they never heard of the name even; and if by chance they should hear of it, they only grin at it, and repeat gamesome stuff about 'spouters' and 'blubber-boilers,' and such like pretty exclamations.

"But what is a *Gam*? You might wear out your index finger running up and down the columns of dictionaries, and never find the word. Dr. Johnson never attained to that erudition; Noah Webster's ark does not hold it. Nevertheless, this same expressive word has now for many years been in constant use among some fifteen thousand true-born Yankees. Certainly, it needs a definition, and should be incorporated into the Lexicon. With that in view, let me learnedly define it: *Gam*. Noun. A social meeting of two (or more) whaleships, generally on a cruising-ground; when, after exchanging hails,

---

[1] Chapter LIII, *Moby-Dick.*

they exchange visits by boats' crews: the two captains remaining, for the time, on board of one ship, and the two chief mates on the other. . . .Of all ships separately sailing the sea, the whalers have most reason to be sociable—and they are so. . . .For the long absent ship, the outward-bounder, perhaps, has letters on board; at any rate, she will be sure to let her have some [news]papers of a date a year or two later than the last one on her blurred and thumb-worn files. And in return for that courtesy, the outward-bound ship would receive the latest whaling intelligence from the cruising-ground to which she may be destined, a thing of the utmost importance to her. And in degree, all this will hold true concerning whaling vessels crossing each other's track on the cruising-ground itself, even though they are equally long absent from home. For one of them may have received a transfer of letters from some third and now far remote vessel; and some of these letters may be for the people of the ship she now meets. Besides, they would exchange the whaling news, and have an agreeable chat. For not only would they meet with all the sympathies of sailors, but likewise with all the peculiar congenialities arising from a common pursuit and mutually shared privations and perils . . . .[2]

"There is another little item about Gamming which must not be forgotten here. All professions have their own little peculiarities of detail, so has the whale fishery. In a pirate, man-of-war, or slave ship, when the captain is rowed any-

---

[2] In the following analyses a "gam" will be construed as an encounter with another whaler, whether or not it turns out to be a time of actual sociability.—Author's note.

where in his boat, he always sits in the stern sheets on a comfortable, sometimes cushioned seat there, and often steers himself with a pretty little milliner's tiller decorated with gay cords and ribbons. But the whale-boat has no seat astern, no sofa of that sort whatever, and no tiller at all. High times indeed, if whaling captains were wheeled about the water on castors like gouty old aldermen in patent chairs.

"As for a tiller, the whale-boat never admits of any such effeminacy, and therefore as in gamming a complete boat's crew must leave the ship, and hence as the boat steerer or harpooneer is of the number, that subordinate is the steersman upon the occasion, and the captain, having no place to sit in, is pulled off to his visit all standing like a pine tree. And often you will notice that being conscious of the eyes of the whole visible world resting on him from the sides of the two ships, this standing captain is all alive to the importance of sustaining his dignity by maintaining his legs. Nor is this a very easy matter; for in his rear is the immense projecting steering oar hitting him now and then in the small of his back, the after-oar reciprocating by rapping his knees in front. He is thus completely wedged before and behind, and can only expand himself sideways by settling down on his stretched legs; but a sudden, violent pitch of the boat will often go far to topple him, because length of foundation is nothing without corresponding breadth....It would never do in plain sight of the world's riveted eyes, it would never do, I say, for this straddling captain to be seen steadying himself the slightest particle by catching hold of anything with his hands; indeed, as token of his entire buoyant self-command, he generally carries his hands in his trowsers' pockets; but perhaps being generally very large, heavy hands, he carries them there for ballast. Nevertheless there have occurred instances, well-authenticated ones too, where the captain has been known for an uncommonly critical moment or two, in a sudden squall, say—to seize hold of the nearest oarsman's hair, and hold on there like grim death."

By describing the role of the captain in such detail Melville underscores the dignity of a whaling captain's position and his own cognizance of it. In the gams of *Moby-Dick* only once can we imagine Ahab taking up this position, when he deigns to go to visit the *Samuel Enderby* because his curiosity about Captain Boomer's maiming overcomes his reluctance to bring attention to his own handicap. Nevertheless, Ahab's dignity is reflected in the attitude of his crew towards him. They are willing to obey him and, in the end, to care for him—and even go down with him.

3

The Pequod Meets the *Albatross*[1]

"Southeastward from the Cape, off the distant Crozetts, a good cruising ground for Right Whalemen," the *Pequod* sighted her first sister-whaler, the *Albatross* from Nantucket.[2] After four years of being at sea, the Albatross was finally heading home. Usually this was cause for jubilation aboard a whaler, but not for this ship. She gave every appearance of desolation. Her sides were coated with rust, and her spars and rigging seemed to be covered with hoar-frost. The men of the crew were wild, unkempt, and forlorn-looking. As Ishmael describes them, "They seemed clad in the skins of beasts, so torn and bepatched the raiment that had survived nearly four years of cruising."

The first question shouted to the *Albatross* by the *Pequod*'s lookout was, according to Ahab's standing order, "Ship ahoy! Have ye seen the White Whale?" Strangely, the lookouts of the *Albatross* did not answer. Nor did they respond to the repeated hearty hails of the *Pequod*'s quarterdeck—"Ship

---

[1] Chapter LII of *Moby-Dick*.
[2] The Crozetts are islands southeast of the Cape of Good Hope.

ahoy! Have ye seen the White Whale?"—but returned only apathetic stares. The captain himself seemed afflicted by the same strange apathy, for in his attempt to call to the *Pequod* as she sailed past, he was unable to hold his trumpet to his lips, for "it somehow fell from his hand into the sea." When he did bestir himself to try to make himself heard without his trumpet, the wind rose and made his efforts vain. But Ahab seized his own trumpet and loudly called out, defiant and sure,

"Ahoy there! This is the Pequod bound round the world! Tell them to address all future letters to the Pacific Ocean!—and this time three years, if I am not at home, tell them to address them to—"

He did not have time to finish, for the ships were sailing rapidly apart. As their wakes crossed, shoals of small fishes, up to now friendly companions of the *Pequod*, darted away from her side in apparent terror and ranged themselves close to the *Albatross*. This small happening, a common sight to sailors, moved Ahab to a strange, "deep, helpless sadness," such feeling as he had not shown before. Did he then have a presentiment of his fate? Were the forces of Nature ranged against him? Yet in the next moment he was crying out to the steersman in his defiant "old lion voice," "Up helm! Keep her off round the world!"

He is once again Ahab, master of his fate, captain of his soul. At least, that is what he tells himself. Not only that, but he believes that he is master of the souls of his crew as well.

Melville at this point impinges upon the scene (in the person of Ishmael) as he leaves the narrative vein and becomes philosophical while musing upon the dubious wisdom of Ahab's decision to "round the world." He asks—and answers his own question:

Round the world! There is much in that sound to inspire proud feelings; but whereto does all that circumnavigation conduct? Only through numberless perils to the very point whence we started, where those that we left behind secure, were all the time before us.

Were this world an endless plain, and by sailing eastward we could forever reach distances, and discover sights more sweet and strange than any Cyclades or Islands of King Solomon, then there were promise in the voyage. But in pursuit of those far mysteries we dream of, or in tormented chase of that demon phantom that, some time or other, swims before all human hearts, while chasing such over this round globe, they either lead us on in barren mazes or midway leave us whelmed.

In his portrayal of the gam of the *Albatross* Melville's artistry in painting an unforgettable word picture is striking. With frugal strokes of the pen he creates a mood of bleak hopelessness compounded with overtones of foreboding and tragic defiance. As was usual in *Moby-Dick*, the names Melville chose for the ships encountered by the *Pequod* on her long and ill-fated voyage could have allegorical implications.[3] His keen interest in English literature is reflected in an obvious intent to evoke an aura of mystery, desolation, sorrow, and possibly guilt, such as Samuel Taylor Coleridge awakens in his "Rime of the Ancient Mariner," which also deals with the enigmatic qualities of the sea and its indelible effect upon those who choose the seafaring life.

Why Melville pictured a ship named *Albatross* in such a dismal way leads us to consider the nature of the albatross, which has been immortalized by Coleridge and also consider

---

[3] The name "Pequod" refers to a tribe of Indians annihilated by New England colonists.

the situation which parallels that in which the Ancient Mariner found himself. The popular assumption suggested by the *cliché*, "an albatross around my neck" is that an albatross represents a vexatious burden which has come upon the victim through no fault of his own. However, Coleridge shows the albatross to be a benign creature who, if welcomed, brings good fortune to the sailors on board a ship in the form of fair winds, for the boon is always related to natural phenomena. If not welcomed, its mistreatment—it was killed in the "Rime"—brings guilt and retribution upon the irresponsible wrongdoer, as happened to the penitent Ancient Mariner. "God save thee, ancient Mariner /From the fiends, that plague thee thus!—/Why look'st thou so?" could have been addressed to the dejected captain of the *Albatross* and to his miserable crew. [4]

Can we derive from this parallel that Melville sees the nature of primeval life (the albatross) as in essence good, but that it is transmuted by humanity's iniquities into evil and suffering (the burden of the dead albatross upon the guilty Mariner)? There is no indication here that the captain of the *Albatross* himself has been guilty of killing an actual albatross during his long voyage—no reason is given for his forlorn aspect: Melville's meaning might be sought on a different level. It is significant that Melville chooses to describe the first gam as a depressing, disheartening experience for the erstwhile jovial crew of the *Pequod*. Even the reader is not unrea-

---

[4] In "The Whiteness of the Whale" Melville (or Ishmael) describes seeing a wounded albatross on the deck of a ship, one which had been caught by a sailor with a "treacherous hook and line." He wonders at its mystical qualities.

sonable in hoping for a cheerful encounter for the crew of Ahab's outward-bound whaler, for they have years of loneliness to endure, as the *Albatross* had. But here Melville is consistent in his resolve to be a realist, even at the expense of his compassionate readers.

This first meeting of two sister-whalers is representative of an attitude which is echoed throughout the encounters that follow; it is a paradigm of all the relationships under Ahab's control, whom Melville, in this initial ship-to-ship encounter, calls "the insane old man," thus intimating that Ahab was not blameless in the abortive gam of the *Albatross*. Melville makes this more explicit as he writes candidly:

> The ostensible reason why Ahab did not go on board of the whaler was this: the wind and the sea betokened storms. But even had this not been the case, he would not after all, perhaps, have boarded her—judging by his subsequent conduct on similar occasions—if so it had been that, by the process of hailing, he had obtained a negative answer to the question he put. For, as it eventually turned out, he cared not to consort, even for five minutes, with any stranger captain, except he could contribute some of that information he so absorbingly sought.[5]

Since Ahab's attitude constituted an intentional exploitation, not a sharing, he was destined never to know the warmth of a relationship as the *Pequod* followed its "pre-ordained" course, and perhaps the *Albatross'* captain's knowledge of this discouraged him from persisting in a friendly approach which would be rejected, for Ahab's reputation was bruited far and wide among whaling captains, especially those from Nantucket, as this captain was. Later on we see

---

[5] From Chapter LIII, "The Gam."

how Starbuck, not as worldly-wise as the captain of the *Albatross* and thus hopefully clinging to a belief to the last that he could appeal to Ahab's common sense and understanding, shared the general destruction because he would not see that immutable Ahab was beyond the reach of human help. Starbuck had greater insight than either Stubb or Flask, but he refused to admit that the obsession in Ahab had finally eclipsed all other emotions.

Throughout the novel the gams of the whalers represent the humane values possible in a voyage that otherwise sets premium upon stoicism and brute strength. Possibly Melville wishes to show that the captain of the *Albatross* realized, after Ahab's abrupt rejoinder, that the only value for Ahab lay in his determination to conduct his seafaring for his own purposes, without acknowledging his kinship with others who, he is convinced, are to be exploited rather than respected as fellow human beings on the same merciless voyage.

Usually Melville is not so direct in indicating the symbolic nature of his writing, but here he places the picture directly before us with his own commentaries.[6] These we can define as we will by imagining the drama of the two ships slowly and for the most part silently crossing paths. We can see the crews of the two whalers which have come so close that the six men on the rigging "might almost have leaped from the mastheads of one ship to those of the other." It would have seemed most natural for the men to hail each

---

[6] Frank Jewett Mather, Jr. notes this quality in Melville: "Melville finds a suggestion or a symbol in each event and fearlessly pursues the line of association." In "Melville's Masterpiece," *New York Review*, I (August 9, 1919).

other, especially since one ship was homeward bound from its long voyage (at least they survived), and the other was embarking on the same challenging enterprise. Even though the *Albatross* was homeward bound, it still had thousands of miles to go to get back to Nantucket, as a glance at a world map will reveal. This makes Ahab's refusal to allow his crew to share a gam even more callous. Outgoing whalers usually had letters and newspapers to give to the ships they might meet on the homeward voyage, but only once, in the meeting with the *Jeroboam*, is it noted that Ahab remembered this courtesy—and then it was too late, for the addressee had already drowned.

In the unpleasant encounter with the *Albatross* is suggested the unresponsiveness in most human relationships, sometimes on the part of one, sometimes on both parts. The men of the *Pequod* would have hailed their fellows, but the apathy evinced by the *Albatross'* crew effectively denied their kinship, and no contact was established, not even when a common purpose—the hunting of whales—could have formed a bond. A notable fact in this encounter is that the *Pequod's* crew was cheery and hopeful, being on their outward journey, this in contrast to the weariness of the men of the *Albatross* who were marked by the hardships and terrors of a four-year whaling voyage.[7] Their ship is a testimony to the pitiable state into which man, his powers vitiated by time and trouble and perhaps a futile chase after "demon phantoms," can sink. Their wreckage symbolizes the toll that the

---

[7] It will be seen throughout the *Pequod's* strange voyage that the men of the *Pequod* do not lose their heartiness in spite of their many discouragements.

difficulties of life, demanding adjustment and re-adjustment, take from the human spirit, which may become as benumbed and unresponsive as that of the men of the *Albatross*.

The languid captain, too, is part of this forlorn symbol: he seems to have lost hope that communication can be effected. Even his half-hearted efforts to hail his fellow captain are negated by circumstances—such as the wind that blows his trumpet into the sea—and his own inability to make himself heard without it, even though the two ships are not far apart. Yet perhaps he should not have been so discouraged—if he had noticed it, the ranging of the little fishes alongside his ship might have given him new hope, signalling, perhaps, that Nature could favor him. This, a small happening in Nature, was given importance by Melville as he shows that its portent was not lost upon Ahab, even though he was determined not to heed the warning. Nothing was going to obstruct his search for revenge against the White Whale, to whom he attributes malice—in fact, he is to Ahab malice incarnate.

With this first implication of an indictment of Ahab's attitude , Melville may have had in mind the lesson, learned through many tribulations, which the Ancient Mariner impressed upon his unwilling listener, the wedding guest.

We shall see that Ahab's punishment is greater than the Mariner's, for he is unrepentant and therefore destroyed. The captain of the *Albatross* survives, like the Ancient Mariner, to carry his burden of penitence. Even so, forgiveness may be possible for him; for Ahab there will be annihilation.

4

The *Town-Ho's* Story[1]

In great contrast to the apparent simplicity of the meeting of the *Albatross* and the *Pequod*, Melville offers us in the second gam a long and complex tale of intrigue and adventure which the crew of the *Pequod* learned about from their harpooneer, Tashtego, in spite of his having been sworn to secrecy:

> For that secret part of the story was unknown to the captain of the Town-Ho himself. It was the private property of three confederate white seamen of that ship, one of whom, it seems, communicated it to Tashtego with Romish injunctions of secresy, but the following night Tashtego rambled in his sleep, and revealed so much of it in that way, that when he was wakened he could not well withhold the rest.

Ahab himself had not left the *Pequod* for a gam with the captain of the *Town-Ho*, but he had generously allowed some of his crew to go aboard for an extended gam, a welcome reprieve after the lonely months at sea. We know at least that Ishmael and Tashtego were among the fortunate ones. This favor was granted because Ahab had already received "strong news" of Moby Dick—which was, it turned out, that

---

[1] Chapter LIV.

the *Town-Ho* had lost a man to the White Whale—so, of course, it was evident that Ahab's quarry was in those waters. Thereafter in this episode all we are told of Ahab is that he never learned of the secret part of the tale which Ishmael and the others heard.

Although Tashtego confided this secret to his shipmates on the *Pequod*, it was withheld from the quarterdeck, that is, Ahab and the officers. But Ishmael was one of those who did learn of this strange secret.

It is actually Ishmael who relays the tale of the *Town-Ho* within this gam, introducing it with the equivocal remark, "For my humor's sake, I shall preserve the style in which I once narrated it at Lima, to a lounging circle of my Spanish friends, on one Saint's Eve, smoking upon the thick-gilt tiled piazza of the Golden Inn."[2] But the chronology of these events is not clear. There are more ambiguities in this gam than in any other. A portion of the "secret part" of the story told by the crew of *Town-Ho* concerned "Radney," who figures in the story Ishmael later relates to his "Spanish friends." Radney was in one of the *Town-Ho*'s boats which had lowered for Moby Dick: he was never again seen after the sailors had attacked Moby Dick and then lost him as he eluded their harpoons. Was Radney swallowed by the whale? All that was seen of him after the struggle were the red tatters of his shirt.

---

[2] In 1843 Melville spent a year as an ordinary seaman on the frigate *United States*, during which time the squadron to which it was attached spent considerable time off the shores of Peru. His *The Piazza Tales* (1853-1858) are based on his experiences there.

No doubt this stirred a superstitious fear in Tashtego's listeners on the *Pequod*, as Melville notes:

> So potent an influence did this thing have on those seamen in the Pequod who came to the full knowledge of it, and by such a strange delicacy, to call it so, were they governed in this matter, that they kept the secret among themselves so that it never transpired abaft the Pequod's main-mast.[3]

Melville emphasizes the element of mystery by using such words as "obscure," "secret," "unknown," "strange," "secrecy", and "Romish."[4] Another aspect of the "secret part" of the story is sometimes interpreted as being Moby Dick's "intentional" killing of Radney, ostensibly to save Steelkilt from having to do so. But why this should be kept from the quarterdeck is not clearly explained. Captains and officers can share knowledge of "judgments of God which at times are said to overtake some men," as Melville describes them. Ishmael, ambiguous as ever, is not certain that the rumor is true: according to him, "it is said" that it was so. Steelkilt became ringleader of a mutiny, but the sequel to his adventures after leaving his beleaguered ship was known to only a few—among them Ishmael.

Later, Ishmael would interweave this "darker thread" with a story he told in Lima, Peru, to some "Spanish friends." So we have in the *Town-Ho's Story* a many-layered narration, with mystery to be piled upon mystery. The story Ishmael tells us has become an oft-repeated tale (with the "dons" the

---

[3] That is, Ahab and the officers never learned about it.

[4] Referring to the mysterious intrigues often practiced by the Church of Rome of earlier times.

fourth in line to hear it, probably with permutations, and we readers the fifth), but as we shall see, he swore to its veracity (ambiguously) "in substance and in its great items" (and no more than that).

Trying to put Ishmael's seagoing career in an orderly perspective is not so easy as it would have seemed when we first saw him signing on to the *Pequod* that Christmas Day in Nantucket. A note of ambiguity is interjected here, too, as we wonder how much time had elapsed between the *Pequod's* disaster, with Ishmael's rescue by the *Rachel*, and his landing in Peru? Did he ship out on another whaler, or was he merely "visiting" friends he had known before his stint on the *Pequod*? We see Ishmael in a new dimension, one that is not elucidated anywhere else in the novel, and a multitude of questions come to mind.

Thus there is much to create a mood of doubt, secrecy, complexity, and exotic unreality, and of "fatality" as well. Ishmael enhances this mood, too, by showing that his Peruvian friends are not entirely convinced of the truth of his story. Asks Don Sebastian:

> "I entreat you, tell me if to the best of your own convictions, this your story is in substance really true? . . . Did you get it from an unquestionable source?"

Ishmael affirms, of course, that he swore on the "Evangelists" that it was, according to his conviction, "in substance and its great items, true" because he had talked with Steelkilt since the death of Radney:

> "I trod the ship, I knew the crew; I have seen and talked with Steelkilt since the death of Radney."

The emotions evoked by the *Town-Ho's* story within a story are as intricate as the narrative. This tale is a microcosm of the troubled complex of conflicts in human relationships. The tangled events described by Ishmael mirror the incalculable complexity of these relationships as the characters move from personal relations (Radney and Steelkilt) to relations within and among groups of the mutineers (before and after their betrayal of Steelkilt) and the loyal sailors, from relations with government (the captain and the mutineers) and back again to personal relations (between Steelkilt and the captain after Steelkilt successfully mutinies). What is significant, too, is that there is hardly a pleasant emotion in the whole narrative. Even the joking of Steelkilt which infuriates Radney, the only bit of humor to be found, has an undertone of sadism and resentment.

To accept the *Town-Ho's* story as a paradigm of human relationships is to raise for oneself a myriad of disquieting questions. They concern the reality which underlies human behavior, even the nature of the driving force of life itself. These questions concern the freedom of the individual and the possibility of man's doing anything to improve his condition, if, as Freud maintains, "a powerful measure of desire for aggression has to be reckoned as part of [man's] instinctual endowment."[5] Although he pre-dates Freud, Melville has a "startling prescience. . . about the unconscious," comments Willard Thorp.[6]

---

[5] Sigmund Freud, *Civilization and Its Discontents* (London: Hogarth Press, 1949), 85.

[6] See his introduction to *Melville: Representative Selections* (New York: American Book

Throughout the tale Ishmael reiterates the idea that the actions of man—here only evil acts—are pre-ordained. The narrative is chilling and depressing with its burden of cruelty, hatred, malice, anger, calculation, violence, perfidy, betrayal, and exploitation. The implication that these are pre-ordained, not because of an external force, but because of the necessities of human nature, is most disconcerting to those who cling to a belief in man's perfectibility. Melville seems to believe that what determines man's fate are "not so much predictions from without, as verifications of the foregoing things within. For with little external to constrain us, the innermost necessities in our being, these still drive us on."

Radney was "doomed and mad" in his baiting of Steelkilt: he was "predestinated" in his actions, for "the fool had been branded for the slaughter by the gods." Steelkilt, in his turn, plotted murder in his "fore-ordaining soul," but his revenge was consummated vicariously, for "by a mysterious fatality, Heaven itself seemed to step in to take out of his hands into its own the damning thing he would have done": it was Moby Dick who became the vehicle for Steelkilt's revenge.

Because the killing of Radney was accomplished without Steelkilt's complicity, again Ishmael (or is it Melville?) suggests that "a strange fatality pervades the whole career of these events, as if verily mapped out before the world was charted." So even Fate itself (or Heaven) can "will" acts of destruction, according to this perception of the universe. Steelkilt, who has flaunted all the rules of so-called civilized

Company, 1938), lxxxi.

behavior, becomes the victor, as if Fate is not interested in retribution for hurtful actions. The question remains, however: was Steelkilt guilty because he had willed Radney's death? Similarly, we have asked if the captain of the *Albatross* was guilty of something which he had not done.

The *Town-Ho*'s story, then, illustrates one conception of human nature by articulating the spiritual chaos in which man moves and has his being. If this story is reliable, how could there ever be any harmony in human life? It is a depressing outlook indeed, but can we assume that it is Melville who tells us that this is so? Would he have agreed with Freud or not? To take the story at face value as a narrative purporting to be based upon fact would lead us to believe so. But on another level we may reflect that Melville has framed Ishmael's *Town-Ho* narrative in single, double, and even triple quotation marks. Melville, the author, thus makes himself a remote observer, just as the reader is, in this portrayal of Ishmael's reminiscences about murky adventures in the company of some "Spanish friends," telling this tale of the chaotic nature of human relationships as they very often occur, but not always in such a dramatic form.[7]

By this indirect method Melville may be hinting that although this lamentable condition of things is so usual that most of us take it for reality, it might not necessarily reflect the innate truth of what is possible—it is actually "foreign,"

---

[7] Ishmael's friends tell him that "Lima" is a byword for unusual corruption, and it is the they, natives of Lima, who can hardly believe Ishmael's story without incontrovertible proof, perhaps because they are so used to living with falsehood.

as are many of the details of Ishmael's narration. By the state of doubt and ambiguity in which he places us at the very start of the story and by the exotic flavor of the scene in which Ishmael relates it—in an aristocratic group of foreign friends in a foreign town in a fanciful Golden Inn in a gilded setting—Melville heightens the impression of remoteness and artificiality, and creates a drama to which we need not lend credence unless we are credulous. Using this approach, which is as intricate as the tale of the *Town-Ho* itself, Melville may be trying to communicate to us his belief that extreme pessimism concerning man's ability to live with man in harmony is not the final attitude which should be taken, that such attitudes are, or should be, "foreign" to our nature.

The *Albatross* has presented a picture of despair and defiance; the *Town-Ho* makes the reasons for despair and defiance palpable in the context of typical human motivations but leaves us to ponder a multitude of ambiguities. In the next gam Melville ranges the themes of responsibility and order beside those of madness and chaos. Can the individual effect control, or will fate thwart every effort?

5

The *Jeroboam's* Story [1]

"**H**and in hand, ship and breeze blew on," and one day the *Pequod* sighted another whaler. On this occasion it was the *Pequod* which set its signal for the other ship when it was still quite a distance away.[2] It turned out that it was the same *Jeroboam*, also from Nantucket, once mentioned by the *Town-Ho's* crew, so we are told—but we have not heard of "Gabriel" before, even though his fame had been carried over the seas far and wide. If that was the "secret part" of the story bandied about by the crews of the *Town-Ho* and the *Pequod*, the reader had been kept in the same ignorance as the quarterdecks of the two ships. But now we are about to be enlightened, we think.

In response to Ahab's signal, the captain of the *Jeroboam* descended into his small craft and was rowed over alongside the *Pequod*, but he refused to go aboard, explaining that his ship was being visited by an epidemic, to which he did not

[1] Chapter LXXI

[2] Melville explains that whaling captains can identify each other by special signals which are set down in captains' books for that purpose.

wish to expose others. Ahab, however, was not deterred by this startling piece of information and urged his fellow captain to come aboard. "I fear not thy epidemic, man," were his words, words which again reflect his lack of concern for the welfare of his crew when he had hope of getting news of Moby Dick. Captain Mayhew, more sensitive than Ahab, insisted upon remaining in his own boat, and their conversation was carried on in this manner.

Pulling an oar in the *Jeroboam*'s boat was an unusual-looking man.

> He was a small, short, youngish man, sprinkled all over his face with freckles, and wearing redundant yellow hair. A long-skirted, cabalistically-cut coat of a faded walnut tinge enveloped him; the overlapping sleeves of which were rolled up on his wrists. A deep, settled, fanatic delirium was in his eyes.

Immediately Stubb recognized him as Gabriel, the mad sailor whom he had heard about during the gam with the *Town-Ho*, and exclaimed loudly, "That's he! that's he!"

At the moment of Captain Mayhew's arrival alongside the *Pequod* all attention except Ahab's was drawn to Gabriel, who was shouting imprecations over the crashing of the waves. In his madness, as the crew of the *Pequod* knew, the eccentric sailor, having convinced the men of the *Jeroboam* that he was a prophet, proclaimed himself to be the archangel Gabriel. Through his crazed ravings he had struck fear and terror into the hearts of the crew, especially when he had prophesied the death of the chief mate of the *Jeroboam*, which occurred when he had insisted upon lowering for Moby Dick in spite of Gabriel's thundering forecast of certain doom. Without regard for the authority of the captain (whom he had invited to quit his own ship), Gabriel arrogated to himself control of the *Jeroboam* and held the crew under his spell:

> He published his manifesto, whereby he set himself forth as the deliverer of the isles of the sea and vicar-general of all Oceanica. The unflinching earnestness with which he declared these things; the dark, daring play of his sleepless, excited imagination, and all the preternatural terrors of real delirium, united to invest this Gabriel in the minds of the majority of the ignorant crew, with an atmosphere of sacredness.[3]

Captain Mayhew had planned to drop this "scaramouch" off at the nearest port for the sake of discipline, but the rebellious crew threatened to mutiny if he should be ousted from the ship. When the plague broke out, the terrorized men gave Gabriel credit for even greater powers of prophecy, so much so that now he was in undisputed control of the ship. Melville anticipates our skepticism of such happenings on board a ship by commenting:

> The sailors, mostly poor devils, cringed, and some of them fawned before him; in obedience to his instructions, sometimes rendering him personal homage, as to a god. Such things may seem incredible; but, however wondrous, they are true. Nor is the history of fanatics half so striking in respect to the measureless self-deception of the fanatic himself, as his measureless power of deceiving and bedevilling so many others.

---

[3] Melville, with his great interest in Europe, especially Britain (where Karl Marx lived in exile), might have been aware that the first edition of the "Communist Manifesto" was published by Marx and Friedrich Engels in 1848. Perhaps he was thinking of "false prophets" in this connection, for although he was a critic of the American economic system, he had no desire to see it destroyed in a bitter class struggle, which he thought could be avoided by the good will of the industrialists, if they had any.

Ahab's interest in Captain Mayhew had been aroused because he had reason to think that he could gain some information about Moby Dick from him—ordinarily, as we well know, he did not welcome a fellow-captain, even one from Nantucket, as Mayhew was. This time Ahab was not disappointed, for Captain Mayhew had news of the White Whale and it was a "dark story" of tragedy. He tried to relate it, but Gabriel, ignoring his captain's orders to be quiet, interrupted him all the while, excitedly screaming that in his very presence, and in spite of his warnings, the mate of the *Jeroboam* had been sent to his ocean-grave by the very White Whale which Ahab was seeking.

Thus Gabriel got ahead of his captain with news of the chief mate's death, but Captain Mayhew persisted in telling his version of the "dark story." Afterward, however, he was amazed at Ahab's reaction. This strange captain of the *Pequod* merely importuned him with further questions about Moby Dick, as if the story had made no impression upon him at all! Puzzled, Mayhew asked Ahab if he was planning to chase the White Whale in spite of everything he had heard. Ahab came back with a resounding "Aye!" This infuriated the demented sailor, whom Ahab was intentionally ignoring. In his rage he pointed an ominous finger at Ahab and screamed, "Think, think, of the blasphemer—dead, and down there! Beware of the blasphemer's end." But Ahab, said Melville, "stolidly turned aside." What Gabriel called "blasphemy" was Ahab's refusal to acknowledge his prophecies which he was convinced were of celestial origin, vouchsafed to him by God himself.

Enhancing the sense of tragedy surrounding the chief mate's death is the episode of a letter which the *Pequod* was carrying for the *Jeroboam*, in case the two ships should meet. Melville explains the customary role of whalers in carrying news from home:

> Every whale-ship takes out a goodly number of letters for various ships, whose delivery to the persons to whom they may be addressed, depends upon the mere chance of encountering them in the four oceans. Thus most letters never reach their mark; and many are only received after attaining an age of two or three years or more.

In this regard we see Ahab in an unusually mellow mood as he remembers a well-travelled letter he has for the *Jeroboam*, one apparently given him before the *Pequod* left Nantucket. Perhaps he was rewarding Captain Mayhew because he had brought him news of Moby Dick:

> "Captain, I have just bethought me of my letter-bag; there is a letter for one of thy officers, if I mistake not. Starbuck, look over the bag."

Starbuck brought back a letter, "sorely tumbled, damp, and covered with a dull, spotted, green mould . . . .Of such a letter, Death himself might well have been the post-boy." This macabre post-boy could well have brought the letter indeed, for it was addressed to the man who had found death in his battle with Moby Dick. Unreadable as it appeared to be, it was sent down to Captain Mayhew in his boat by means of a long cutting-spade pole. Gabriel, however, objected to the delivery of the letter, screaming a menacing prophecy to Ahab:

> "Nay, keep it thyself. . . .Thou art soon going that way."

> "Curses throttle thee!" yelled Ahab. "Captain Mayhew, stand by now to receive it."

Ironically, it was Gabriel who caught the letter as the wind blew it out of Captain Mayhew's grasp. Defiantly, the mad sailor reloaded the letter on the pole and sent it back to the *Pequod*, where it fell on the deck at Ahab's feet. Before Ahab had a chance to send it back, Gabriel shrieked to his captain's oarsmen to begin pulling and "the mutinous boat rapidly shot away from the *Pequod*." Gabriel had won in a confrontation with yet another superior officer, this time with Captain Ahab himself. Here once more Nature steps in to thwart Ahab to prove that he may be able to command men to bow to his will, but control of Nature, in the form of wind and sea (and the animals within it) is beyond his power, something he does not wish to acknowledge. It would not be long before another of Gabriel's prophecies would come true. What does this say about the proclaimed supremacy of reason?

No reasoning by Captain Mayhew or ranted warnings by Gabriel could sway fearless Ahab. A reasonable fear would have prompted him to avoid the danger of close contact with the captain of the infected ship in the interest of his crew's welfare, even in the interest of the success of his own quest, for an epidemic would surely have frustrated his plans. Irrational fear would have urged him to heed the premonitions of the crazed and cabalistic Gabriel. Against the stormy background of the swelling sea, Ahab stands unmoved in his resolve, his inexorability foreshadowing the words with which he later coldly refused Starbuck's plea to give up the fatal chase, stolidly denying any friendship Starbuck might have felt toward him as he declared:

> "But in this matter of the whale, be the front of thy face to me as the palm of this hand—a lipless, unfeatured blank."

That is how Ahab would view every human being as the months went by and events on the *Pequod* unfolded.

The scene of the *Jeroboam* is significant not only for Ahab's part in it, however. In this gam, too, Melville emphasizes again the differences which separate the men from the officers, for even if there is democracy, there is also a hierarchy of authority. As was pointed out before, the captains and officers of the *Town-Ho* and *Pequod* did not learn the secret part of the story of Radney and Steelkilt. This points to an unspoken agreement among crew-mates not to divulge knowledge which could jeopardize their fellow whalemen. Melville observes after the *Jeroboam*'s boat left and, it is assumed, Ahab went down to his cabin and officers took their stations again:

> As, after this interlude, the seamen resumed their work upon the jacket of the whale, many strange things were hinted in reference to this wild affair.

This delineates the separation between the hands and the officers. Again certain things were going to be kept secret, even from us—all we get are "hints." It is noteworthy that although Ishmael insisted that he had talked to Steelkilt after Radney's death, it appears that the captain of the *Town-Ho* never found mutinous Steelkilt to prosecute him for this serious infringement of the law of the sea, nor would Ishmael admit that he knew his whereabouts. Melville, who had in his seafaring life occasion to know much of this kind of solidarity (since he was a mutinous ringleader himself at one time), notes this characteristic, this "strange delicacy," among the men, as we noted before:

> So potent an influence did this thing [the "secret part"] have on those seamen in the Pequod who came to the full knowledge of it, and by such a strange delicacy, to call it so, were they governed in

this matter, that they kept the secret among themselves so that it never transpired abaft the Pequod's main-mast.

A further significant relationship at the heart of this gam is that of the *Jeroboam*'s crew to their usurping leader, Gabriel. Their irrational devotion to him and his doctrine points up the paradoxical quality in man's nature, a quality which betrays him when he allows fear to conquer his reason. Here impotent reason and the authority needed for the survival of society are represented by the deposed captain and the mates, who seem unable or unwilling to check Gabriel's mutinous actions and end the magnetic hold he has on the crew, just as on the *Town-Ho* the captain seemed strangely intimidated by Steelkilt.

We cannot help asking why Captain Mayhew and his officers were unable to impose the traditional discipline upon the unruly crew. The rules of the sea gave the captain precise prerogatives: he could put the men in irons, flog them or impose any other punishment he deemed necessary, for a captain on a ship at sea, remote from civilization, represented the laws which regulated human relationships on land. We must assume that there was a failure of will, especially on the part of the captain. Because of the rules of the hierarchy, the officers could not supersede him. He was in command. Captain Mayhew revealed his incompetence or insecurity when he did not carry out his decision to drop Gabriel off at the nearest port: could he not have confronted the men and punished the ringleaders after Gabriel had been exiled? Chaos on board the *Jeroboam* was the result of Captain Mayhew's failure to carry out the responsibilities which he as an individual was bound to observe; therefore Gabriel was able to fill the breach with his anarchistic doctrine and fearsome prophecies. This ship was finally visited by a sickness, while the *Town-Ho* lacked even the semblance of order imposed by Gabriel.

We ask what Ahab would have done under the same circumstances, but this is hypothetical, because mutiny did not become a problem on board the *Pequod*, and Ahab was not about to risk it, since that might spell the end of his quest.[4] Were the men loyal because Ahab's will was so strong that the men feared and respected him, or was it because he had held out the promise of the golden doubloon?[5] Ahab had once soliloquized:

> I will not strip these men... of cash, aye cash. They may scorn cash now; but let some months go by, and no perspective promise of it to them, and then this same quiescent cash all at once mutinying them, this same cash would soon cashier Ahab.

Ahab is superior to the other two captains in his psychological approach to his men: he knows how to manipulate them for his own ends. He was so successful that some of his crew had internalized his quest and taken it for their own, while others, as he knew, thought of material gain alone. Yet he did not give them credit for their loyalty: many of them were genuinely devoted to him—Starbuck and Stubb, for example.[6]

---

[4] See "Surmises" for some of Ahab's secret thoughts.

[5] Actually it was Ahab who first saw Moby Dick when the fatal chase was about to begin, and he claimed the doubloon, saying "Fate reserved the doubloon for me," but then in a moment of generosity said he would pay ten times the amount to the lucky man. See "The Chase—First Day."

[6] In regard to his crew Ahab's developed a touch of paranoia. In "The Hat" Melville shows that he was not sure his officers would tell when Moby Dick was sighted, but he "sagaciously" refrained from expressing his doubts, for although

The *Jeroboam*'s message is relevant on the level of the individual. Each member of the crew, because of ignorance or failure to act, has given up his autonomy and has become only a "manufactured man," re-created by the fanatical leader to be merely a "tool" for his ambition. Those who give over their individuality to such leaders, Melville implies, finally are lost in a world of superstition and irrationality. Through Gabriel's magnetic spell the rules of the sea are overturned, rational authority nullified, while madness and violence replace reason. We learn that after the epidemic had broken out on board, Gabriel had more power over the crew's minds than ever before. Fear had increased their hope that Gabriel's magic could save them.

Too, the gam of the *Jeroboam* echoes the theme sounded in that of the *Town-Ho*, that men often need externals to constrain them or they become victims of their own inability to control their instinctive urges and are catapulted into acts of desperation. For this reason civilization has slowly and painfully built up hierarchies of belief and rules of conduct—the bulwark of the collective Freudian *superego* against the primeval *id*. Thus Melville once again points to an unassailable paradox in the human situation.

This gam is replete with intimations concerning the future of a society which is composed of such misled individuals who have become as contemptuous of law as the crewmen of the *Jeroboam*. By tying together the episodes of the *Town-Ho* and the *Jeroboam* through the person of Gabriel,

he boasted that he was independent, he knew that he was dependent upon his whole crew for support in his quest.

who became known both through rumors and his actual presence in the gam, Melville accentuates the actuality of malevolence and chaos in relationships between human beings and their existence within the structures which uphold organized society. As we saw, the tangled skeins of the Radney-Steelkilt story were shot through with venomous emotions which could well preclude the presence of good in any form. Both men were violent, unprincipled, but since they might have been predestined to be that way, are they to blame? Perhaps our only hope is to believe as Starbuck did: that "faith must oust fact," for the notion that good could prevail under such circumstances cannot be proved—what is most palpable is that inner "predestination" seems to be the most potent driving force behind all the afflictions that buffet the hapless characters, who are also beset by chance and ambiguities which cannot be understood.

The calamities which befall the men on the *Jeroboam* carry out this same theme. Their course seems predetermined, for ineffable Fate itself, it appears, steps in to prove that truth is a prerogative of Gabriel. As long as the men believe this, they will never be free of Gabriel's curse. Because reason, of which the quarterdeck is a symbol, cannot suppress Gabriel, the *Jeroboam* is cut off from civilized society, represented by rules of the sea, and they are isolated as well by the epidemic—a phenomenon of Nature which society dreads and avoids. Here it appears as a spiritual contagion which only reason can alleviate. Thus they are completely alienated from their fellows, seemingly condemned to sail the waters until the plague has run its course or everyone has died from it.

Seer though he seems to be at times, Melville could not have imagined the catastrophes to be brought about by demagogues and dictators in the twentieth century, but he had the intuition to sense the possible trend of societies in which man would give up his individuality to become part of the collective will. Suffering from the insecurity caused by a civilization hostile to his emotional needs, man is likely to turn to strong leaders who can reassure him. The problems of humanity seem to change only in degree, not in kind. The situation of those aboard the blighted *Jeroboam* can be likened to that of modern mankind struggling with the fears arising from the potentials of the atomic age, which fears have spread like an epidemic on a global scale.

We do not hear that the *Jeroboam*'s captain was ever successful in ridding his ship of the double scourges of Gabriel and the epidemic. Once again we are left with a dramatic example of unsatisfactory human behavior and modes of thought. Not yet have we encountered a clue to the solving of humanity's personal and social dilemmas. Like the gam of the *Town-Ho*, that of the *Jeroboam* shows us madness and death, both of which haunt the *Pequod*, reflections of the madness and death whose source is the perverse leadership of Ahab.

6

The *Pequod* Meets the *Jungfrau*[1]

The fourth encounter of the *Pequod* takes place with a German ship, the *Jungfrau*, a name which can be translated as "a young woman," or "virgin." This time it is the stranger-ship which initiates the gam. As Ishmael says of the *Jungfrau*'s actions: "While yet some distance from the *Pequod*, she rounded to, and dropping a boat, her captain was impelled towards us, impatiently standing in the bows instead of the stern."

Captain Derick De Deer, whom Melville calls "master" and notes that he was from Bremen, came to the *Pequod* as a suppliant "eager to pay his respects," seeking oil for his lamps.[2] Strange it was that he should be short of the very commodity whose abundance on a whaler was so commonplace. Starbuck was the first to see that the German captain had a lamp-feeder in his hand as he stood in the boat brought alongside the *Pequod* by his oarsmen. But Stubb pretended to misunderstand:

---

[1] Chapter LXXXI

[2] The notion of virgins without oil to light their lamps comes from *Matthew*, chapter 25, of the New Testament.

"Not that," said Stubb, "no, no, it's a coffee-pot, Mr. Starbuck; he's coming off to make us our coffee, is the Yarman; don't you see that big tin can there alongside of him?—that's his boiling water. Oh! he's all right, is the Yarman."

"Go along with you," cried Flask, "It's a lamp-feeder and an oil-can. He's out of oil, and has come a-begging."

Captain Derick clambered aboard and was accosted at once by Ahab, who plied him with questions about the White Whale. But the German was interested only in getting his oil-can filled—complaining "in his broken lingo" that every drop of his Bremen oil was gone and he and his crew had to climb into their hammocks in the dark, for they had been unable to kill a whale to replenish their supply.

There was no lack of generosity on board the *Pequod*, and soon Captain Derick returned to his boat where his oarsmen awaited him. But before he had time to board the *Jungfrau* again, whales were sighted by lookouts from both his ship and the *Pequod*, and "without pausing to put his oil-can and lamp-feeder aboard his whaler, he slewed 'round his boat and made after the Leviathan lamp-feeders"—eight of them had appeared!

> Aware of their danger [the whales] were going all abreast with great speed straight before the wind, rubbing their flanks as closely as so many spans of horses in harness. They left a great, wide wake, as though continually unrolling a great wide parchment upon the sea.

This made the sea the more dangerous for the pursuing whalemen. Both contenders decided to chase one large whale, an "old bull," who was slower than the others. Thereupon ensued a fierce competition among four German boats and the boats which the *Pequod* had hastily lowered, for each crew was determined to be the first to land its harpoon. It happened that the German boats had the lead at first because Derick's boat was already in the water, but as one of the *Pequod*'s boats came close to him, with deriding gestures Captain Derick shook his lamp-feeder at his rivals.

"The ungracious and ungrateful dog!" cried Starbuck, "He mocks and dares me with the very poor-box I filled for him not five minutes ago!"

Captain Derick's scornful attitude infuriated Stubb also, for he cried to the men in his boat:

"I tell ye what it is, men....It's against my religion to get mad; but I'd like to eat that villainous Yarman —Pull—won't ye? Are ye going to let that rascal beat ye?"

But Derick was not content to show contempt for his erstwhile benefactors by derisive gestures alone. As he saw the *Pequod*'s boats coming close, their oarsmen goaded on to furious efforts by their anger and Stubb's frantic urgings (and promise of "a hogshead of brandy"), he pitched his lamp-feeder and oil-can into the sea in their path, trying to slow their progress—even to the risk of their capsizing. This was certainly adding insult to injury, and perhaps it was doubly unfortunate, for, who knows? it may have been that which brought the displeasure of Heaven upon him. At the beginning of the contest he had such a decided head start that, in Melville's words,

. . . he would have proved the victor in this race. But after his ungrateful behavior, a righteous judgment descended upon him in the form of a crab which caught the blade of his midship oarsman.

As the "clumsy lubber" strove to free his oar, the *Jungfrau*'s boat lost its initial advantage, and one of the *Pequod*'s boats shot up alongside its rival and closed in on the whale, which was desperate with fright. There is no doubt about Melville's sympathy for the hunted creature:

> So have I seen a bird with clipped wing, making affrighted broken circles in the air, vainly striving to escape the piratical hawks. But the bird has a voice, and with plaintive cries will make known her fear; but the fear of this vast dumb brute of the sea, was chained up and enchanted in him; he had no voice, save that choking respiration through his spiracle, and this made the sight of him unspeakably pitiable.

A German harpooneer rose to throw his harpoon, but "all three tigers" from the *Pequod*—Queequeg, Tashtego, and Daggoo—sprang to their feet in the careening boats and three "Nantucket irons" flew over the heads of their rivals and landed in the whale's body. The intensity of the whale's twisting caused such a tumult of waves that the boats rammed. The German boats were overturned and Derick and his harpooneer were unceremoniously spilled out and "sailed over by three flying keels" of the *Pequod*'s boats. The Germans were left floating on the sea in helpless fury. Such arrogant behavior was contrary to the custom of whalemen, but the enraged men of the *Pequod* were indifferent to their rivals' fate, an action which proves their furious contempt for their deceitful adversaries. Stubb kept his sardonic sense of humor throughout the fray:

> "Don't be afraid, my butter boxes," cried Stubb, casting a passing glance upon them as he shot by; "ye'll be picked up presently—all right—I saw some sharks astern—St. Bernard's dogs, you know—relieve distressed travellers."

With this nonchalant farewell, the *Pequod*'s boats pulled ahead and were victorious in harpooning the coveted whale.

Although the *Jungfrau's* men did survive their ordeal, undoubtedly their foul deeds would be known to all whalemen who plied those waters before too long, and Captain Derick and his crew would be anathema to every other whaler captain and crew.

If Derick's actions represent the amorality and cold ingratitude which are often characteristic of human behavior, then Stubb's remarks may represent the realistic reaction of the pragmatic man. "Dog eat dog," is a crude philosophy which is implicit in Derick's and Stubb's interchange; it is one which is generally condoned in the interest of self-preservation. After all, we could hardly expect Stubb to let Captain Derick's men catch the whale without countering their aggression. If our kindness is flaunted in our face, if we are thought stupid or gullible for our generosity, Stubb would reason, we do not show untoward anger nor seek a revenge beyond that which is appropriate to the situation. Derick and his crew got their "just deserts" because a "righteous judgment" came upon them, and all Stubb did was his duty as a good whaleman acting within his rights, which did not preclude leaving the "Yarmans" in the cold sea to save themselves as best they could. So might reason practical Stubb, and at a superficial level, the level of the everyday struggle for survival, he seems to be right.

There is no pretense between the crews of the *Jungfrau* and the *Pequod*; as they clash, primeval forces, exemplified by the sea and the vagaries of chance (the "clumsy lubber's" bad luck is crucial) come into play. Each man is strong; no one asks for pity or indulgence. The forces they battle against are strong and merciless, too. Man pitted against man in the need to wrest from Nature the wherewithal to sustain himself—

this is the age-old dilemma of mankind and the incubus from which pure evil can arise. Captain Derick's reactions were amoral, savage (not in the sense of being wild, but of being undeveloped); Stubb's response was amoral and also savage, as was Flask's as well.

This gam again brings up the question of the true nature of man's inner self. The name of the ship, the *Virgin*, implies a state of innocence in human relations. but in view of the actions of Captain Derick, this seems to mean that even seeming innocence is sullied by the darker elements of human nature—in other words, there is no innocence. Would this be related to the theme of original sin? Or, in Freudian terms, we can say that the *id*, which knows no morality, is concerned only with the satisfaction of its own drives at any cost. The most noticeable quality of the contacts of Stubb and Derick in this gam is their amorality, or lack of moral responsibility. Not to be overlooked, moreover, is the assumption that this amorality is condoned in the practical world.

Melville tells us that the state in which God places man is savagery. But where in the gam of the *Jungfrau* shall we find the non-savage? There seems to be one example: Starbuck, he who had filled the "poor-box" for the "Yarman" suppliants. And in the subsequent description of the killing of the whale it is noteworthy that Melville refers to Starbuck as "humane," while Flask is called "cruel" for his uncalled-for brutality toward the whale as they strove to kill it. The theme of Starbuck's compassion is carried out in "The Musket" where the first mate is shown in the throes of indecision about the wisdom of killing Ahab to save the crew from death, but he cannot bring himself to commit this "inhumane" deed. Melville points up Starbuck's greater sensitivity, but one must reason on several levels, including the extremes of the levels of sheer realism and pure Christian ideals, to decide whether or not Starbuck is therefore wiser as the world would judge him.[3]

The characterization of Starbuck is central to the gams, for it is he who carries on the consistent theme of morality. That he holds to a religious philosophy of life is brought out in "Merry Christmas," when an "old rigger," a rough sailor who has signed up on the *Pequod* for another voyage, tells Ishmael that Starbuck "is a lively chief mate, that; good man, and a pious. . . ." Yet he is respected by all, even Ahab, for his skill, courage, and intelligence. Nor was he afraid to face Ahab down when he felt that it was his duty to do so.[4]

On the part of the German crew evil was returned for good, and there was no question of the *Pequod's* immediate response: the "Yarmans" were paid in their own coin, and as a result they came up bankrupt, floating on the sea with no one to help because of their perfidy. The ethical question here is, "Did the *Pequod's* crew do right by refusing to save their fellow whalemen from possible drowning?" Fortunately, they were saved by chance from this fate, and the ethical dilemma remains unaddressed.

---

[3] Melville was greatly influenced by Shakespeare, to whom Camus compares him for the lyricism of his style, here the *Hamlet* comparison becomes obvious.

[4] See "Ahab and Starbuck in the Cabin." A question of reasonable procedure in the ship's maintenance was the issue. Whenever Starbuck figures in the novel, he appears as one with humane qualities rather than one who is a character "given stock jobs to do, set speeches to make", as suggested by R. P. Blackmur in "The Craft of Herman Melville," included in *American Literary Essays*, edited by Lewis Leary (New York: Thomas Y. Crowell, 1960).

Melville presents a starkly realistic picture of human relationships. The most noticeable quality of the captain and crew of the *Jungfrau* is their amorality, in other words, a total lack of moral sensitivity and responsibility. Emphasized, too, is the fact that this amorality is condoned in the practical world of affairs by the pragmatic man who finds justification in its evident objectivity. Starbuck, however, is shocked at Captain Derick's ingratitude; the more violent reaction of the others, voiced by Stubb, is that of anger and desire for revenge.

In spite of the fact that this gam is lightened by humor, it is evident that we should not quickly assume that Melville would have us look in this direction to find a suitable guide to the handling of the predicaments of life, whether they be in the workaday world, as shown in the actions of this gam, or in spheres which more closely touch our personal lives. Although in his seafaring life he had probably witnessed just such behavior many times, as an observer we may be sure that without judging his shipmates too harshly, he felt that there must be a better way. But what?

7

The *Pequod* Meets the *Bouton de Rose*[1]

One day as the *Pequod* was "slowly sailing over a sleepy, vapory, mid-day sea. . .the many noses on the. . .deck proved more vigilant discoverers than the three pairs of eyes aloft."

> "I will bet something now," said Stubb, "that somewhere hereabouts are some of those drugged whales we tickled the other day. I thought they would keel up before long."

As the *Pequod* advanced, a ship showing French colors became visible. Alongside she was carrying a "blasted" whale, one which had been wounded by another ship and which had died, or perhaps one which had died a natural death and had been found floating on the sea. The odor from these whales, as Ishmael declares, is "worse than an Assyrian city in the plague when the living are incompetent to bury the departed." (The name *Bouton de Rose*, or *Rose Bud*, of course, provides a touch of Melvillian humor—"this was the romantic name of this aromatic ship.") Ordinarily, whalers do not pick up such whales, but evidently the captain of the French whaler was not aware of this whaling custom since he lacked

[1] Chapter XCI

experience, having been a Cologne manufacturer before taking to the sea. (Another touch of Melvillian humor.) If this captain were aware of his blunder, only cupidity made him decide to attempt to bring the blasted whale in—but since this was his first voyage, it is assumed that he was merely ignorant of whaling traditions.

As the *Pequod* drew closer to the *Bouton de Rose*, it was seen that she carried a second whale alongside, and this one "seemed even more of a nosegay than the first." Stubb again nonchalantly reveals his Yankee prejudice against foreign whalemen as he calls the French sailors "Crappoes" (from *crapaud*, "toad," perhaps also showing disdain for their eating of frogs). Harking back to the metaphor of the *Jungfrau*'s "poor-box," Stubb, ever the humorist, suggests that since the French whalemen are "but poor devils in the fishery," someone ought to pass 'round a hat so that the *Pequod* might make the *Rose Bud* "a present of a little oil for dear charity's sake."

The gam which follows brings us a drama which is similar in vein to that of the *Jungfrau*, with certain variations. The general theme is carried in part again by Stubb, whose "righteous cunning" upon this occasion earns him one of the most valuable treasures a whaleman can find—ambergris.

Throughout the narrative Melville makes mention of Stubb's deliberate deceit toward the men of the *Rose Bud*. As he perceives the stranger-ship's rather humorous predicament (at least he finds it so), with two apparently unusable whales alongside, Stubb muses:

> "Now that I think of it, it may contain something worth a good deal more than oil; yes, ambergris. I wonder now if our old man has thought of that."

As usual, the "old man," Captain Ahab, was interested only in whether the *Rose Bud* had encountered Moby Dick during her voyage, and he gave Stubb permission to visit her if first he should enquire about the White Whale. Obediently, Stubb and his mates went out in their boat to ask that question and at the same time to satisfy Stubb's curiosity about the activities on board the odorous French whaler. The becalmed *Pequod* was left behind "fairly entrapped in the smell, with no hope of escaping except by its breezing up again."

Approaching the *Rose Bud* from the starboard side, Stubb held his nose and shouted, "*Bouton de Rose,* ahoy! are there any of you Bouton-de-Roses that speak English?" Although Stubb could not understand the inscription "*Bouton,*" on the ship's bows, the bright red and green carved figure of a rose made it plain that the ship's name was a flowery one.

Luck had it that there was one, the chief mate, "the Guernsey man,"—so named because he was from the island of Guernsey—who could speak English. From him Stubb learned that the *Rose Bud*'s crew were unaware of the existence of such a creature as a White Whale. Stubb ordered his boat back to the *Pequod* to where Ahab was eagerly waiting:

> Rapidly pulling back toward the Pequod, and seeing Ahab leaning over the quarter-deck rail awaiting his report, Stubb moulded his two hands into a trumpet and shouted, "No, sir! No!" Upon which Ahab retired, and Stubb returned to the Frenchman.

Thereafter the picture takes on a garish hue, as if Melville wished to mirror the tawdriness of the little planned deceits which cheapen human relationships. "The fanciful French taste" with which the ship was ornamented—incongruous for a whaling vessel—lends an air of tarnished elegance to the scene. Even the name *Bouton de Rose* itself, along with the nationality of the ship, was likely to invoke a certain disdain, if not amusement, since things French were looked upon from a Nantuckers' perspective as being effete (especially by rough-and-ready American whalemen). This spectacle is made even more unpleasant by the atmosphere of disorder and discord in which the *Rose Bud*'s crew was unwillingly working, since the repulsive smell of the blasted whales offended their senses. As Ishmael observes, "They worked rather slow and talked very fast." Their labors were not to be rewarded by the pulling-in of a whale caught in heroic combat but wasted on a malodorous, futile drudgery, for the crew knew that oil from such a whale would be of inferior quality and thus would bring little material gain.

When Stubb returned to the French ship the chief mate was talking excitedly in French in an attempt to persuade his captain to let the dead whales go. Much more of that disgusting work and they might have a mutiny on their hands, he feared. But the captain was adamant in his refusal to loose them. Stubb, of course, was interested in making a "loose fish" of at least one of the whales by maneuvering the captain into ordering a halt to the work of hauling the "booty" fast to the ship (Melville calls it a "nosegay"), because once a whale was loosed, according to the customs of whaling, Stubb would be within his rights to explore it for precious ambergris.

Stubb cannily refrains from letting the mate know what is on his mind. In his turn, the mate, with Stubb's connivance, deceives the captain by mistranslating Stubb's English words, telling the captain that Stubb is warning about the possibility of the crew's becoming sick with fever from the diseased whales. In this effort Stubb and the Guernsey man are supported by the ship's surgeon, a Frenchman who, after "outcries and anathemas," has taken himself into his *cabinet* on the deck when his strong objections to the work on the blasted whales were ignored by the inexperienced captain.

While the Guernsey man is slyly misconstruing Stubb's warnings to the French captain, Stubb contemptuously refers to the captain with insults, such as, "Tell him for me that he's a baboon," basking in the knowledge that the captain cannot understand a word he says and will accept all in good faith, as long as he smiles and smiles and plays the villain! By his actions, Stubb pretends to work for the crew's benefit as he joins in the dispute between the captain and his clamorous mate, but Stubb is actually coveting ambergris, if any exists in the *Rose Bud*'s whales.

Everyone's purpose is finally accomplished as the alarmed captain is persuaded to rid the ship of the offending whale for fear of epidemic, and Stubb, after one "fast fish" becomes a "loose fish," has his oarsmen tow it back to the *Pequod*. As the *Rose Bud* prepares to sail away, in the shelter of the *Pequod*'s hull Stubb looks for the prized ambergris, which to his glee he discovers by the handfuls.[2] Possibly Stubb, cheered on by his fellow crewmen, could have obtained more, but stern Ahab commanded him to return, or the *Pequod* would sail without him. It is likely that Stubb believed

---

[2] Chapter XCII is devoted to a description of the social uses of ambergris, including as an ingredient in perfumes, noticeable "when a musk-scented lady rustles her dress in a warm parlor," the parlor, of course, being in dramatic contrast to the stormy sea where the whales are killed.

Ahab would do it, too: it seems that he did not delay in getting back to the *Pequod.*

If all ends happily, and everyone is satisfied (the French captain is even grateful), why should we assume that Melville is criticizing the social actions in this gam? After all, now the *Rose Bud's* captain will probably be more discerning and will find another whale acceptable to his crew. He could not resent Stubb's good fortune since he, a neophyte whaling captain, probably was unaware that some whales contain the precious ambergris. Stubb acted legally, not even displaying eagerness until the whale had become fair game for anyone. This was his "righteous cunning" in action again.

Why was it not perfectly acceptable for him to take advantage of the captain's inexperience, even to appropriating the ambergris for himself? Stubb once again acts on the practical level, using covert aggression. This has been explored in the preceding gam, the encounter with the *Jungfrau,* when he used overt aggression to reach his goal. We feel satisfied that we have discovered the philosophic source of Stubb's behavior—a socially condoned expediency, touched with greed, is at the base of his actions.

Stubb's personality is well-delineated in this gam to complement other descriptions of him which are found throughout the novel. "Stubb's Supper," is a revealing chapter, as is "First Night-Watch," when we come across a rare soliloquy—but it is short and direct, as befits a man like Stubb.

Though he is not a reflective man, Stubb has evolved his own "easy answer" to the problems of life: a laugh—along with the notion that Fate (or perhaps chance?) is the final arbiter:

"Ha! ha! ha! ha! hem! clear my throat!—I've been thinking over it ever since, and that ha, ha's the final consequence. Why so? because a laugh's the wisest, easiest answer to all that's queer; and come what will, one's comfort's always left—that unfailing comfort is, it's all predestinated. . . .I know not all that may be coming, but be it what it will, I'll go to it laughing."[3]

Moreover, Stubb is not filled with idealistic longing to be with his wife (assuming he is married) as Starbuck is. Though he has a "true love" back on shore, he has no illusions about her faithfulness as his thoughts turn homeward:

"What's my juicy little pear at home doing now? Crying its eyes out?—Giving a party to the last arrived harpooneers, I dare say, gay as a frigate's pennant, and so am I!"

We should also take note of Ahab's conduct in regard to the *Rose Bud*, for much of the action hinges upon Ahab's lack of concern for the predicament of his fellow captain who, it appears, needed assistance, or at least advice, from a more experienced whaling master. Instead, he allows the social relations to fall into anarchy, since Stubb, who takes charge, has no more fellow-feeling than Ahab. Perhaps the Cologne manufacturer does not even know of the custom of gamming.

Yet can blame be attached to Stubb's actions? Unlike Ahab, he did not have the social or the moral responsibility, perhaps not even the desire, to attend to the courtesies of the gam in place of Ahab, who instead of taking on this responsibility, departs from the quarterdeck. Moreover, Ahab exhibits

---

[3] Stubb's last speech, in "The Chase—Third Day," combines self-pity, defiance, and acceptance.

indifference to the gathering of the ambergris. He has only one thought: to find out where the White Whale is.

"Am I my brother's keeper?" is answered here in the negative once again as Ahab and the *Pequod* journey farther on the path of social alienation. Can we assume that either pattern of conduct is wrong: that of Stubb's legalism or Ahab's aloofness? Again we are left in doubt.

8

The *Pequod* Meets the *Samuel Enderby of London*[1]

The gam of the *Samuel Enderby* differs from the other gams in *Moby-Dick* up to now because here for the first time during the voyage Ahab left the *Pequod* to board another ship. But this action was not motivated by friendliness, to be sure. Ahab stayed in character: he sought only news of Moby Dick. This the captain of the *Samuel Enderby* could supply, for in a struggle with the White Whale he had lost an arm.

As soon as the *Samuel Enderby*, bearing English colors, hove on the horizon, Ahab took his position on the quarterdeck and when the stranger-ship was within hailing distance he took up his trumpet and called out, "Ship ahoy! Hast seen the White Whale?"

The captain of the English ship did not have to call back. He merely lifted a "white arm of sperm whale bone, terminating in a wooden head like a mallet."

Upon such a tempting rejoinder Ahab was fired with zeal to board the stranger–ship. "Man my boat!" he ordered. In

---

[1] Chapter C.

less than a minute Ahab's willing oarsmen had brought him alongside the English ship.[2] In his haste and excitement, however, he had forgotten that no other ship but the *Pequod* was equipped with the mechanical contrivance which permitted him, since he had lost a leg to Moby Dick, to clamber aboard a vessel for gamming. Proud Ahab suffered humiliation for a moment as he eyed the ladder swung down for him by the sailors of the *Samuel Enderby*:

> So, deprived of one leg, and the strange ship of course being altogether unsupplied with the kindly invention, Ahab now found himself abjectly reduced to a clumsy landsman again, hopelessly eyeing the uncertain changeful height he could hardly hope to attain.

> It has before been hinted, perhaps, that every little untoward circumstance that befel him, and which indirectly sprang from his luckless mishap, almost invariably irritated or exasperated Ahab. And in the present instance, all this was heightened by the sight of the two officers of the strange ship, leaning over the side, by the perpendicular ladder of nailed cleets there, and swinging towards him a pair of tastefully-ornamented man ropes, for at first they did not seem to bethink them that a one-legged man must be too much of a cripple to use their sea bannisters.

But this humiliating impasse lasted only a moment, because almost at once the tactful captain took note of the situation and ordered down the cutting tackle, enabling Ahab to be hoisted aboard, for, as Melville tells us, "they had had a whale alongside a day or two previous, and the great tackles were still aloft." However, Ahab did not allow himself to be

---

[2] Melville tells us in "The Gam" that it was customary for the second ship to send over a complement of crewmen to enjoy a gam, but in this episode it seems that only Ahab paid a visit, for we hear nothing of the English crew's reciprocal gamming.

drawn up supinely, for he also helped energetically "by pulling hand over hand upon one of the running parts of the tackle."

Almost immediately the subject of conversation was Moby Dick, for the two captains had something in common: maiming by the White Whale. Melville emphasizes this shared experience by calling the chapter "Leg and Arm," referring to the welcome the captains gave to each other—an extremely friendly act on Ahab's part, but then he thought he had something to gain:

> With his ivory arm frankly thrust forth in welcome, the other captain advanced, and Ahab, putting out his ivory leg, and crossing the ivory arm (like two sword-fish blades) cried out in his walrus way, "Aye, aye, hearty! let us shake bones together! an arm and a leg! an arm that never can shrink, d'ye see, and a leg that never can run."

Ahab wanted to know how the Englishman had lost his arm: "Spin me the yarn!" he exclaimed eagerly. "How was it?"

> "It was the first time in my life that I ever cruised on the Line," began the Englishman.[3] "I was ignorant of the White Whale at that time."

As the story unfolded Ahab learned that Captain Boomer had tangled with Moby Dick and had seen harpoons embedded near his "starboard fin." "Aye, aye—they were mine, *my* irons!" exulted Ahab, his vengeful thoughts rushing back to that fateful day when he and Moby Dick had struggled, and

---

[3] The "Line" refers to the Equator.

he had lost. But now he knows that Moby Dick was maimed, too. He will never be rid of Ahab's harpoons—they are as much a talisman of the battle as Ahab's ivory leg.[4] This evens the odds of the coming competition when Moby Dick's haunt is found.

Captain Boomer went on to describe his terrible sufferings as Moby Dick attacked him and "swallowed" his arm. Dr. Bunger chimed in sympathetically (and banteringly as well), giving details of that baneful day. But Ahab's next words were, "What became of the White Whale?"—he was tired of all that irrelevant talk about pain and sufferings. When he found out that Captain Boomer had lost all interest in challenging Moby Dick again, Ahab in turn lost interest in the Englishman and was ready to leave, all pleasantries, such as they were, at an end.

During the conversation which intervenes between the welcome and the leave-taking, Dr. Bunger casts meaningful glances at the ivory arm of one and the ivory leg of the other captain. And when Ahab insists, in spite of all he has heard and seen on board the *Samuel Enderby*, that he will push his pursuit of Moby Dick until the bitter end, Dr. Bunger anxiously exclaims, "This man's blood—bring the thermometer—it's at the boiling point!"

In his concern for Ahab Dr. Bunger quickly brings forth his thermometer to take his temperature, for mariners were always concerned about fevers which might be signs of the plague. But Ahab rudely dashes him against the bulwarks

---

[4] We read later that Moby Dick has many harpoons embedded in him, some of them rusting away.

and peremptorily commands the ship's sailors to lower him
into his own boat. It is significant and not surprising that
Ahab breaks the communication, although "communication"
is rather too strong a word for an exchange to which Ahab
brings so little, expressing as he does only impatience at the
solicitous warnings and friendly demeanor of the Englishmen.
These for Ahab meant only a delay in getting the details
of the subject which obsessed him. It appears that Ishmael, at
least, disapproved of Ahab's curt actions toward Captain
Boomer, who seemed to be the personification of that hospitality
for which Ahab returned only disdain. In "The Decanter,"
Ishmael notes that when he was sailing off the
Patagonian coast, he had had a "fine gam" on the *Samuel
Enderby*, when he had enjoyed some "noble, solid Saxon hospitality.
. .long after old Ahab touched her planks with his
ivory heel." We can assume from this that Ishmael was in the
boat which rowed Ahab to visit the English whaler, since he
knew everything which took place and could relate it to his
own later experiences. This observation, too, gives further
insight into Ishmael's activities after his rescue from the disaster
of the *Pequod*.

As Ishmael remembers, the atmosphere on board the
Samuel Enderby was English—not as on an English merchant
ship, but somehow as in an English home, simple and dignified,
in contrast to the fanciful *Bouton de Rose*.

> . . .The Samuel Enderby was a jolly ship, of good fare and plenty;
> fine flip and strong, crack fellows all, and capital from boot heels to
> hat-band.
>
> But why was it, think ye, that the Samuel Enderby, and some other
> English whalers I know of. . .were such famous, hospitable ships,
> that passed round the beef, and the bread, and the can, and the

joke; and were not soon weary of eating, and drinking, and laughing? I will tell you. The abounding good cheer of these English whalers is matter for historical research.[5]

Thereupon Ishmael digresses into this "historical research," none of which would have any relevance for Ahab but which sheds some light upon Ishmael's pleasanter adventures before or after he sailed on the gloomy *Pequod*.

This feeling of good nature and relaxation was imparted to Ahab's visit by the badinage between the captain and his surgeon, Dr. Bunger, who between them represent for Melville the general English character, one the heart, or emotion, and the other the head, or reason. Captain Boomer was adventuresome, even given at times to "diabolical passions," and fearless. But he could control his emotions to a great extent. His self-discipline allowed him to desist from the chase when Moby Dick had divested him of one arm—he will not tempt the formidable whale with the other. He lowered for him only once, he said, and that was enough; Captain Boomer's nature is not vindictive: he is not bent upon revenge as Ahab is. Boomer remarked wryly,

> "He's welcome to the arm he has, since I can't help it, and didn't know him then; but not to another one. No more White Whales for me."

This speech is in great contrast to Ahab's words when Captain Boomer asks him if he doesn't agree that Moby Dick is "best let alone," as he glances at Ahab's ivory leg. "He is," agrees Ahab astutely but at the same time drives home with

---

[5] Ishmael's remarks in "The Decanter."

the same questions about where he can find the White Whale:

> "But he will still be hunted for all that. What is best let alone, that accursed thing is not always what least allures. He is all magnet! How long since thou saw'st him last? Which way heading?"

Thus Ahab enunciates one of the most paradoxical phenomena of human nature: its perverseness, a trait which Melville explores at length throughout this novel. This is a trait which we do not find in Captain Boomer, and his disciplined emotion in regard to Moby Dick is shared by Dr. Bunger, who takes this attitude not because of a disastrous experience of his own, but because his reason tells him how foolish it is to chase a killer whale in view of Captain Boomer's suffering, and, of course, in view of Ahab's experience, too, now that he has met him. After all, there are many other whales to be chased and caught. But that is not the way Ahab viewed it: he left the *Samuel Enderby* as energetically (but in an angrier mood) as he had boarded it.[6]

> In a moment he was standing in the boat's stern, and the Manilla men were springing to their oars. In vain the English Captain hailed him. With back to the stranger ship, and face set like a flint to his own, Ahab stood upright till alongside of the Pequod.

Ahab's refusal to answer Captain Boomer's farewell hail and his stubborn turning toward his own ship foretell his future actions in relation to the rest of the ships he would

---

[6] Ahab suffered for his intemperate behavior, as Melville shows in "Ahab's Leg," which chapter, too, divulges a "secret."

encounter. This was the last time he would leave the *Pequod* to meet a fellow captain.

Nothing could touch Ahab, not the hospitality proffered him, not the common calamity which he and Captain Boomer shared, not the physician's concern for his welfare, not even the captain's kindness in easing his humiliation by quickly improvising a way for him to board the *Samuel Enderby*. He has decided upon his course, and neither fear nor love can sway him. At this point he feels, indeed, as he will say, "I am the Fates' lieutenant."

Now it is evident that Ahab has progressed—or regressed—so far along the path to self-imposed rejection of his fellow man that he can callously strike another for attempting to help him. This gam more than any other so far makes plain Ahab's indifference to deep emotion, except for his passion to wreak vengeance upon Moby Dick. As "Fate's lieutenant," it appears, Ahab had taken charge of the mission of hastening his own destruction.

9

The *Pequod* Meets the *Bachelor*[1]

In the Japanese Sea the *Pequod* met the *Bachelor*, a Nantucket ship ready to start homeward full of rejoicing, for she had "just wedged in her last cask of oil and bolted down her bursting hatches."

> And now, in glad holiday apparel, [she] was joyously, though somewhat vain-gloriously, sailing round among the wide-separated ships on the ground, previous to pointing her prow for home.

On the quarterdeck mates and harpooneers were dancing with the "olive-hued" Polynesian girls who had eloped with them; three Long Island Negroes made music for their dance with the "barbarian sound" of their enormous drums and fiddle-bows of whale ivory. The captain of the *Bachelor*, beaming with satisfaction, stood watching, enjoying the celebration, for the focus of the "hilarious jig" was the excited action around the huge try-pots in which their booty from the captured whales had been harvested.[2]

---

[1] Chapter CXV.

[2] See Chapter XCVI, "The Try-Works," and Chapter XCVII, "Stowing Down and Clearing Up" for vivid descriptions of these all-important activities.

Melville's unusually lively and colorful description of the scene on the rejoicing ship provides us with an example of the composite makeup of a typical whaling crew which drew its sailors from all parts of the globe, and signalling this on the *Bachelor* were the flags of many nationalities flying from the rigging.

> The three men at her mast-head wore long streamers of narrow red bunting at their hats; from the stern, a whale-boat was suspended, bottom down; and hanging captive from the bowsprit was seen the long lower jaw of the last whale they had slain. Signals, ensigns, and jacks [large national flags] of all colors were flying from her rigging, on every side. Sideways lashed in each of her three basketed tops were two barrels of sperm; above which, in her top-mast cross-trees, you saw slender breakers of the same precious fluid; and nailed to her main truck, was a brazen lamp.[3]

It was not just success that they were celebrating, it was prodigious success. "While cruising in the same seas numerous other vessels had gone entire months without securing a single whale," but the *Bachelor* had had such luck that its immense supplies of oil were almost too much for the crew to stow away.

Melville makes a stark contrast between Ahab and the cheerful captain of the *Pequod*'s Nantucket counterpart, who was all smiles and eager to share the celebration with a fellow captain:

> Lord and master over all this scene, the captain stood erect on the ship's elevated quarterdeck, so that the whole rejoicing drama was

---

[3] "Midnight, Forecastle" is an unusual example of jollity on the *Pequod* which also features the multinational makeup of the crew. This, however, did not include the officers, and Starbuck was repelled by the sights and sound of the rough revelry.

full before him, and seemed merely contrived for his own individual diversion.

And Ahab, he too was standing on his quarter-deck, shaggy and black, with a stubborn gloom; and as the two ships crossed each other's wakes—one all jubilations for things passed, the other all forebodings as to things to come—their two captains in themselves impersonated the whole striking contrast of the scene.

It was already too late for Ahab to be persuaded to celebrate another captain's success. Some few weeks before, the harpoon with which he was to make Moby Dick his victim had been welded. The die was cast, and Ahab was no longer a free man. There was no turning back from the eerie scene of "The Forge" when Ahab had uttered the words of the harpoon's fiery baptism: *"Ego non baptizo te in nomine patris, sed in nomine diaboli."*[4] These were words which smacked of blasphemy, which is, of course, what the *Jeroboam*'s Gabriel had warned about—"Beware of the blasphemer's end!"

The quietude of the golden days of those weeks which intervened between the forging of the harpoon and the meeting with the *Bachelor* had seemed to soothe even Ahab. But they had only gilded reality.

Nor did such soothing scenes, however temporary, fail of at least as temporary an effect on Ahab. But if these secret golden keys did seem to open in him his own secret golden treasuries, yet did his breath upon them prove but tarnishing.

Ahab, brooding as he stood on his quarterdeck, morose and silent, could not share the happiness of the other ship. Even returning to Nantucket with a full ship would not make

---

[4] "I baptize thee not in the name of the Father, but in the name of the Devil."

him happy unless he had killed Moby Dick before setting sail for home.

The other captain, however, wanted to dispel the gloom he could sense emanating from the *Pequod*, whose crew we can imagine staring hard and longingly at the other whaler with its deck reverberating with the music and dancing—it would not have taken them long to lower their boats in response to the friendly captain's blandishments.

"Come aboard, come aboard!" cried the Bachelor's commander, lifting a glass and bottle in the air.

"Hast seen the White Whale?" gritted Ahab in reply.

"No; only heard of him; but don't believe in him at all," said the other good-humoredly. "Come aboard!"

But there was no hope of Ahab's relenting. He shot back at the beckoning captain:

"Thou art too damned jolly. Sail on! Hast lost any men?"

"Not enough to speak of—two islanders, that's all;—but come aboard, old hearty, come along. I'll soon take that black from your brow. Come along (merry's the play); a full ship and homeward-bound."

"How wondrous familiar is a fool," muttered Ahab; then aloud, "Thou art a full ship and homeward-bound, thou sayst; well, then call me an empty ship and outward-bound. So go thy ways and I will mine. Forward there! Set all sail, and keep her to the wind!"

And thus, while the one ship went cheerily before the breeze, the other stubbornly fought against it; and so the two vessels parted.

Here we have another surprising contrast: Ahab seeming to be concerned about the lives of crew members, and the complacent, friendly captain sloughing off the death of two men as nothing at all. Why Ahab asked at all is hard to explain. Did he have a foreboding that if he did lower for Moby Dick he might lose some of his men? That he should care seems out of keeping with what we have learned of him, except for the few times when he seemed to relent, especially with Starbuck. But a true softening of his heart would never take place. Ahab displays an attitude of callousness and exploitation toward strangers, but this pattern is carried over into his behavior toward his own crew, for whom he should have felt, if there were any spark of comradeship left within him, some sense of kinship. But no. The cruel pattern is unbroken. In one of his soliloquies, this time in "Surmises," his cynicism and cold calculation toward even those closest to him are clearly revealed as Melville records Ahab's musings:

> Nor was Ahab unmindful of another thing. In times of strong emotion mankind disdain all base considerations; but such times are evanescent. The permanent constitutional condition of the manufactured man, thought Ahab, is sordidness. Granting that the White Whale fully incites the hearts of this my savage crew, and playing round their savageness even breeds a certain generous knight-errantism in them, still, while for the love of it they give chase to Moby Dick, they must also have food for their more common daily appetites. . . . I will not strip these men, thought Ahab, of cash, aye cash. They may scorn cash now; but let some months go by, and no perspective promise of it to them, and then this same quiescent cash all at once mutinying them, this same cash would soon cashier Ahab.

These secret thoughts emphasize the contempt in which Ahab held his men, for as is brought out in "The Ship," Ishmael discovered that the men on whaling ships received very little in cash to compensate them for their hard labors. As proof of this, when Flask was about to drown in the last disaster, he exclaimed to Stubb,

"Oh, Stubb, I hope my mother's drawn my part-pay ere this; if not, few coppers will now come to her, for the voyage is up."

It is characteristic that Ahab did not give his men credit for their loyalty. Some of them were genuinely devoted to him, especially Starbuck and Stubb (in his rough way). But his madness deprived him of empathy and drove him into an emotional isolation which he actually welcomed, although he seemed to regret it in moments of self-pity.

This gam is short and seems simplest of all. In the commonplace, everyday language of friendliness, the *Bachelor* offers the men of the *Pequod* surcease from their unremitting toils and boredom, a new outlook: everything is all right; we lost two men on our whaling cruise, but that's nothing to mourn about—they were only islanders, after all. We're not remembering our tragedies—we're going home with a ship full of oil—come and join the celebration of our good fortune!

The encounter with the gaily bedecked ship presents a colorful contrast to the gray pictures of most of the other gams, but it, too, carries its own undertones of grimness. Although it is assumed that a bachelor represents freedom from the anxieties of responsibility, not all is happiness, even on the good ship *Bachelor*. The crew appears light-hearted, in spite of the death of two islanders, drowned while chasing the whales which had provided them with the over-abundant oil for the ship's casks. The revellers close their eyes to the troubles which follow them, choosing instead to think only of the pleasures of the moment. They will not think of the next voyage—not yet. Melville had said in *Mardi*:

> Though all evils may be assuaged, all evils can not be done away.
> For evil is the chronic malady of the universe, and checked in one
> place, breaks forth in another.

Observing the customary sea rites, the *Bachelor* had already paid sorrowful (though brief) respects to her lost crew mates and had stoically accepted the fact that violent death is a possibility to which all whalemen are exposed, that they themselves are expendable and may be sacrificed at another lowering. Meanwhile, they are not constrained from accepting the pleasures which a capricious Fate allows them. This philosophy does not need the rationale of a driving purpose. It comes to terms with life, even if on an uncritical level, and accepts the paradoxes of existence, just as Stubb, Flask, and Queequeg do.[5] Their attitudes may be contrasted to those of the crew of the *Delight*, which is met later.

The meeting with the *Bachelor* highlights the picture of Ahab which was so unmistakably portrayed upon the deck of the *Samuel Enderby*. One may see in Ahab's refusal to share the *Bachelor*'s joys, and to let his crew do so, a contempt for the joyous philosophy which, though superficial, brings a certain consolation in the face of life's hardships and griefs, one which surely would be less disastrous than the steely mindset to which Ahab had hardened himself. Scorning friendship once again, this time not a "noble," formal hospitality but a carefree invitation to merrymaking, Ahab shows his usual contempt for his fellow man by his words, "How wondrous familiar is a fool!" Embracing his emotional nihil-

---

[5] Chapter CX, "Queequeg in His Coffin," illustrates this very well.

ism and his alienation from others, he declares, "Call me an empty ship and outward-bound."

Although the gam of the *Bachelor* is very short, the jocose captain and his happy crew provide the most colorful relief on the voyage so far. More could have been said about the reaction of the *Pequod*'s crew: surely they were disheartened when the cheerful ship disappeared over the horizon. But it is almost as if a corner had been turned, a door had been closed, all opportunities were at an end.

This encounter does not merely repeat the earlier image, for it reveals a new dimension to Ahab's personality as he stands there in his loneliness. Of himself Ahab thinks, "Ahab stands alone among the millions of the peopled earth, nor gods nor men his neighbors."[6] Leaning over the taffrail, he eyed the homeward-bound *Bachelor* noisily moving away from him, then took from his pocket a small vial of sand. As he held it in his hand meditatively he looked from the slowly vanishing ship to the vial, seeming thereby to bring two remote associations together. That vial was filled with Nantucket soundings. This is a surprising revelation: Ahab carrying a souvenir of remembrance and affection! Perhaps regretting that he has allowed the *Bachelor* to sail away without exchanging visits, Ahab is becoming aware of his hardheartedness toward his fellow-captain—and to his crew? Not likely: he is already aware of that, as he has said many times.

Ahab may be briefly regretting the golden past when he was a stalwart, proud, unmaimed whaling captain, and he

[6] This takes place on the first day of the chase for Moby Dick.

may be regretting having lost the family life which, according to others, he once enjoyed. This is doubtless what the vial represents. But this breath of warm emotion, this sentimentality, is entirely in keeping with his character, with the rigid personality which he has displayed all during the voyage. His sentimentality is essentially based on the self-love and self-pity which relate to the image which he has of himself. Holding in his heart an ideal conception of himself as fundamentally noble and loving, he rationalizes that it is a magnetic force, an irresistible power, Fate, which keeps him from love. The vial of native sand reinforces his conviction that he is indeed a good husband and father and that he could have been like other men if only Fate had not ordained otherwise. In this manner he eschews responsibility for his hard-heartedness toward his crew and toward fellow whalemen whom he meets on the vast sea.

Thus self-pity relieves Ahab of the burden of guilt which he carries with him, as the Ancient Mariner did. He perceives with his intellect that his conduct is not without blame (as he discloses later with the *Rachel*'s coming), for he risks taking other men to their death for his desperate undertaking, but he cannot experience, or cannot allow himself to experience, the emotion that would make any other conduct possible for him.

At times this inability to feel emotion made Ahab anxious, almost angry as he exclaimed in "The Sunset" while standing alone watching the horizon,

"This lovely light, it lights not me; all loveliness is anguish to me, since I can ne'er enjoy. I lack the low, enjoying power; damned, most subtly and most malignantly! damned in the midst of Paradise!"

The tender moments which Ahab reveals at times have no real meaning for others because they serve only as his relief from the feelings of guilt which pursue him. These seemingly tender feelings are rooted, as all his emotions are, in egocentricity: Fate is against him—he can feel it; Moby Dick was the instrument of his maiming: that set the pattern of Nature's spite against him, even to the token abandonment of the little fishes who left him for the *Albatross*, making him sad.

Later on Ahab again reveals this sentimentality and self-pity in "The Symphony" as he talks with Starbuck just before the chase for Moby Dick begins. He says many things which perhaps he realizes are true: that humane values are much more important than the primordial ones to which he has given his life and which hold him in thrall. Mistakenly, Starbuck thinks that Ahab's musings represent a desire to change the harsh decision to pursue Moby Dick at all costs. He feels emboldened to beg his captain to turn the ship back to head for Nantucket, where they can once again enjoy the gaiety to match that of the *Bachelor*. Ahab's words give Starbuck reason to hope that Ahab, his mood mellowed by the loveliness of the luminous day, will agree. As they talk about their wives and children back in Nantucket Ahab seems to share Starbuck's desire for relationships with others, especially when he exclaims, seemingly overcome with emotion:

> "Close! stand close to me, Starbuck; let me look into a human eye;
> it is better than to gaze into sea or sky; better than to gaze upon
> God. By the green land; by the bright hearth-stone! this is the magic
> glass, man; I see my wife and my child in thine eye."

Ahab has seen his wife and child in the "magic glass" of Starbuck's eyes that night when Starbuck thought he could dissuade Ahab from the fatal chase, but in vain. Ahab's tenderness focuses upon himself as he brings back memories of the life he has led; but he is not truly sympathetic with the young wife and child he has left alone in Nantucket, no more than with the crew he will lead to destruction, although his words would bring one to think so, as Starbuck thought in those last hopeful moments. Ahab moved inexorably to his habitual rationalizations: his heart was already hardened back to its accustomed steel. Starbuck should have seen this at once, for in spite of the mellowness of his words Ahab had shown what his true decision was. Yet he was capable of an unusual gesture of kindness: he told his first mate not to lower when he did when Moby Dick was sighted:

> "No, no; stay on board, on board!—lower not when I do; when branded Ahab gives chase to Moby Dick. That hazard shall not be thine. No, no! not with the far away home I see in that eye!"

Rejecting Starbuck's last plea to change course, Ahab averted his glance as "like a blighted fruit tree he shook, and cast his last, cindered apple to the soil." With his final words he cast the blame for his misery into the lap of Fate and "crossed the deck to gaze over on the other side." But Starbuck had not heard him. Despairing, he had already silently stolen away. Throughout the voyage it had not seemed to Starbuck that Ahab could be so inexorable; nor did Starbuck try to understand Ahab's obsession:

> [Starbuck] in his soul, abhorred his captain's quest, and could he, would joyfully disintegrate himself from it, or even frustrate it.[7]

---

[7] In "Surmises."

Ahab knew very well how little the quest meant to his first mate. Did this infuriate him—to be subject to the disdain of a man who was closer to him than any other? Was Ahab exploiting Starbuck's emotions: purposely to raise his hopes only to dash them, to muse upon the lost blessings of family life merely to arouse pity for himself in Starbuck's heart?—or even to gloat because Starbuck could do nothing to change his own destiny? No matter what it was—Starbuck felt even more shattered after these moments with Ahab, for he could no longer believe that he could touch Ahab. Nevertheless, he must have touched him: Ahab had only three boats lowered for the final chase; he gave the command of the *Pequod* over to Starbuck, ostensibly to save him. But Moby Dick rammed the *Pequod* and caused it to sink. Fate would not even allow Ahab to carry out his desire to be magnanimous toward the one man who deserved it most.[8]

The disappearance of the rollicking *Bachelor* into the mists of the Japanese Sea represents for the crew of the *Pequod* the disappearance of hope. They are left with the unmitigated cruelty of Ahab's inexorable will. Their future is as hopeless as the cindered apple which fell from the blighted tree.

---

[8] A critical encounter between Ahab and Starbuck is described in Chapter CIX, "Ahab and Starbuck in the Cabin."

10

The *Pequod* Meets the *Rachel*[1]

THE story of the *Rachel* is the most poignant of all the gams of the *Pequod*. It is with this episode that the crescendos of Ahab's violence toward the *Samuel Enderby* and his scornful harshness toward the *Bachelor* come to a dramatic climax.

Here we see a captain of a sister-ship—Captain Gardiner was a Nantucketer whom Ahab knew—coming with a request which in all humaneness is one which cannot be refused: he asks Ahab to help him look for his son, who may at that moment be drowning, along with his mates, clinging to the wreckage of a boat which had been lowered to chase a whale. This whale had been none other than Ahab's nemesis and quarry, Moby Dick.

The two captains hailed each other with questions nearest their hearts: Ahab—"Hast seen the White Whale?" and his friend—"Aye, yesterday. Hast ye seen a whaleboat adrift?"

Ahab gave Captain Gardiner a quick "No!" and hastened to push his own questioning further as the *Rachel*'s captain boarded the *Pequod*. In answer to Ahab's eagerness to know

---

[1] Chapter CXXVIII.

of Moby Dick, Gardiner told his story and ended with his earnest request. It had been Moby Dick which they were chasing, yes, and he was probably still in those waters. It was Moby Dick himself for whom his son and his mates had lowered their boat, and whom they had chased until their boat had vanished from the *Rachel's* sight. Could he but charter the *Pequod* for forty-eight hours so that both she and the *Rachel* could sweep the horizon for some trace of the missing craft, perhaps he might find his son alive. At least, he would know more of his fate if they found that some tragedy had befallen them.

Stubb and Flask watched Ahab breathlessly to note their captain's reaction. "What says Ahab?" cried Stubb to the others. "We must save that boy!" Even they, with all this long, weird voyage behind them, were not prepared for the calculating cruelty of Ahab's reply to the impassioned beseeching of the father who had declared:

"I will not go till you say aye to me. Do to me as you would have me do to you in the like case. For you too have a boy, Captain Ahab—though but a child and nestling safely at home now—a child of your old age, too.—Yes, yes, you relent; I see it—run, run, men, now, and stand by to square in the yards."

But Ahab, who had up to now stood "like an anvil, receiving every shock, but without the least quivering of his own," broke into words for the first time. He ordered his men back.

"Avast," cried Ahab—"touch not a rope-yard!" Then in a voice that prolongingly molded every word—"Captain Gardiner, I will not do it. Even now I lose time. Good-bye, good-bye, God bless ye, man, and may I forgive myself, but I must go. Mr. Starbuck, look at the binnacle watch, and in three minutes from this present instant warn off all strangers: then brace forward again, and let the ship sail as before."

And so saying, Ahab descended to his cabin. Overcome with sorrow at Ahab's unyielding, the father "silently hurried to the side; more fell than stepped into his boat and returned to his ship." The *Rachel* then continued her lonely search, "weeping for her children, for they were not."

As in the gam of the *Samuel Enderby*, Ahab refused to identify himself with a fellow-captain's misfortune; as in the gam of the *Bachelor* he refused to identify himself with the happiness of another fellow-captain, so in this gam of the *Rachel* he refused to identify himself with a fellow-captain's sorrow. "Warn away all strangers," he ordered, demonstrating without a doubt his own attitude toward others. Even a friend from his own Nantucket he calls a "stranger," a friend from that Nantucket whose soundings he kept always with him in a vial, could not move him: now all men to him were strangers. Toward them he felt no sense of responsibility, to share good with them or to share sorrow.

Not only this, but in his passion for self and his devotion to his own obsession, Ahab ignored all feelings of compassion for his crew, saw nothing of his responsibility to them. The "lingering glances" with which his men had followed the merry *Bachelor* as it vanished from their sight had not moved him to grant them the brief social contact to which they were entitled in this long, lonesome journey, no more than was his cold heart moved to allow his crew to act upon the pity they felt toward the unhappy father. "We must save that boy!" Stubb had exclaimed, but his feelings were thwarted by his duty to obey Ahab's heartless command.

The gam of the *Rachel* is an emotional turning point for the men of the *Pequod*. Now they had been forced to relinquish every humane thought, their very souls, to Ahab. Melville describes the finality and foreboding of their plight:

> As the unsetting polar star, which through the livelong, arctic, six months' night sustains piercing, steady, central gaze; so Ahab's purpose now fixedly gleamed down upon the constant midnight of the gloomy crew. It domineered above them so, that all their bodings, doubts, misgivings, fears, were fain to hide beneath their souls, and not sprout forth a single spear or leaf. . . . Alike, joy and sorrow, hope and fear, seemed ground to finest dust, and powdered for the time, in the clamped mortar of Ahab's iron soul.

Here aboard the *Pequod* we see the far-reaching effects of the denial of human rights, the evil of an all-encompassing authoritarianism which rests only upon a neurotic will-to-power. Similarly, by binding themselves into Ahab's service, the crew had given up their liberty, for as the unhappy voyage progressed it grew more evident that Ahab had no sense of moral responsibility, no respect for human dignity. The mysterious Elijah in "The Prophet" had told Ishmael as much before the *Pequod* set sail, just after he and Queequeg had signed up and had filled Ishmael with foreboding:

> "Shipmates, have ye shipped in that ship?" [asked Elijah].
> "Yes," said I, "we have just signed the articles."
> "Anything down there about your souls?"
> "About what?"
> "Oh, perhaps you hav'n't got any," he said quickly. "No matter, though, I know many chaps that hav'n't got any,—good luck to 'em; and they are all the better off for it. A soul's a sort of fifth wheel to a wagon."

We can reason, of course, that the crew who shipped aboard the *Pequod* could not have realized the extent to which their vassalage would go. After all, it was not until much later—in the "The Quarter-Deck"—that Ahab would reveal the true purpose of the voyage. It raises the question of how much critical judgment is required of an individual in any given situation; how much responsibility he must assume for the protection of his own freedom. Evidently the men of the *Pequod* accepted none of this responsibility; they had given it over to Ahab, as Elijah said, when they signed aboard the *Pequod*. When Ahab did finally vouchsafe to them his secret purpose in making the voyage, not one crewman except Starbuck had demurred, so swept away were they by Ahab's fiery and majestic oratory when he announced his vendetta against the whale that had taken his leg:

> I'll chase him round Good Hope, and round the Horn, and round the Norway Maelstrom, and round perdition's flames before I give him up. And this is what ye have shipped for, men! to chase that white whale on both sides of land and over all sides of earth, till he spouts black blood and rolls fin out. What say ye, men, will ye splice hands on it, now? I think ye do look brave."

> "Aye, aye!" shouted the harpooneers and seamen, running closer to the excited old man. "A sharp eye for the White Whale, a sharp lance for Moby Dick!"

Only Starbuck endeavors to dissuade Ahab from the "blasphemy" of his thirst for vengeance "on a dumb brute," but Ahab contemptuously exclaims, "Talk not to me of blasphemy, man; I'd strike the sun if it insulted me." Then cannily he tries to mollify Starbuck and asks him to speak his mind, and getting nothing but silence in return, Ahab says to himself triumphantly, "Starbuck now is mine; cannot oppose me now, without rebellion."

In "Knights and Squires" Melville notes that Starbuck had great courage in meeting the perils of "seas, or winds, or whales," but could not stand up to the "more spiritual terrors which sometimes menace you from the concentrating brow of an enraged and mighty man." Therefore Starbuck was caught in a conflict of values which was now brought to a climax with the appearance of the *Rachel*: he was convinced that Ahab's reckless resolve for vengeance was immoral, but he was committed to loyalty to his captain—he no longer had free choice. As a first mate he would sink to the level of a mutineer if he refused to follow Ahab's bidding, as Ahab well knew. Starbuck would not risk "rebellion," he told himself: the code of the sea superseded moral considerations, for mutiny—putting oneself above the law—was cause for severe punishment, even death. Starbuck had already made his vocal protest in the company of the whole crew: he could go no further in trying to change the behavior of the men under Ahab's command.

Because the first mate was caught in this dilemma, he was reduced to silence, which Ahab gleefully took for compliance. Lacking as he did the right to oppose the captain in any effective way, Starbuck consoled himself with the thought that in time he could yet sway Ahab from his unworthy goal, for occasionally Ahab did manifest some tender feelings, even pity and remorse (if they were not indeed genuine, they did have the effect of confusing Starbuck). When the crucial time came, however, Ahab's flint-like heart would not be deterred from his quest: Starbuck, too, was finally carried on to destruction in the wreck of the *Pequod*.

In the episode of the *Rachel*, then, we see the limitless effects of the evil which arises from the negation of humane values under the domination of a ruthless leader whose powerful will can exert its influence over lesser men; it points out the responsibility of free men to exercise critical judgment in the choice of their leaders. As Father Mapple pointed out, each person has a special mission: woe to him who would do as Jonah had done, "escape his duty and his God by taking ship at Joppa," which is a metaphor for retreating from the confrontation of duty. The message is ambiguous, however, for it can never be known how much of the responsibility belongs to the individual, how much is determined by Fate.

Ahab had vowed to devote himself to one set purpose, and for that he had decided to sacrifice everything else. Yet in his heart he feared that he would not accomplish it, for he saw a mysterious Fate conspiring against him, whether it was in the guise of Nature or in the guise of men such as Captain Gardiner and Starbuck, who called upon the very humanity he had sworn to reject. His first mate, especially, stirred in him feelings of guilt which caused him to exclaim when he refused the grieving captain's pleas: "May I forgive myself!"

In this respect Ahab's actions during the gam of the *Rachel* bring to mind the episode of the *Jeroboam*. We are able here to make a comparison of the two leaders. The theme of madness is broached when two exponents of a deranged mind are juxtaposed: Gabriel the fanatic and Ahab the obsessed. Both have a strong drive to dominate, both succeeded in persuading those around them to work for their own selfish ends. Both are intensely aware of their environment. But Ahab brings an aura of sanity not possessed by Gabriel. Gabriel uses wild intuitions to mesmerize his subjects. Ahab uses men for his domination of Nature and cares nothing for their loyalty to him as long as they are useful. Gabriel's madness was the symptom of a disordered personality which found no definite focus other than a emotionally charged, magnetic will-to-power. Ahab, called obsessively insane, on the other hand, was intellectually aware of his actions; for this reason he was knowingly malevolent. He showed that he understood the effect that his actions could exert upon men when he exclaimed, "And may I forgive myself!" Although both men manipulated their followers through such stratagems as the appeal to superstition, Ahab's was the greater capacity for evil. Greater, too, would have been his capacity for good, while Gabriel, it appears, had no capacity for good, for he could not discriminate between reality and his own delusions. In choosing evil, Ahab chose death for himself and for the others who were under his command.

11

The *Pequod* Meets the *Delight*[1]

Now all is gloom. There is not far to go, for the *Pequod* and its doomed crew are coming close to the haunt of Moby Dick, the waters where some of the crewmen of the *Rachel* have probably perished. But one last ship is seen on their horizon, "most miserably misnamed the Delight." Upon her shears (which on a whaling vessel carry the spare, unrigged or disabled boats) are seen the shattered remains of a whale-boat, its wreckage resembling a "peeled, half-unhinged, and bleaching skeleton of a horse."

To Ahab's question, "Hast seen the White Whale?" the captain, whose gauntness reminds us of the *Albatross*, exclaimed, "Look!" and directed Ahab's gaze to the wreck of the whale-boat. No social exchange would take place here, for the *Delight* had just lost five men. Only one body had been recovered, and at that moment some sailors were busily sewing the corpse into a hammock for burial. This did not deter Ahab. All he wished to know was whether they had killed Moby Dick in their tragic encounter. No! was the reply, and

---

[1] Chapter CXXXI.

the harpoon was not yet forged that would ever do that! But Ahab impetuously held out his own harpoon, the one which had been baptized in his harpooneers' blood and which he had sworn would soon rest behind the White Whale's fin.

Seeing Ahab's fierce determination, the weary captain returned, "Then God keep thee, old man." As his sailors finished their melancholy task, he slowly advanced toward the corpse and breathed a prayer before delivering it into the sea: "May the resurrection and the life. . . ."

"Brace forward! Up helm!" cried Ahab at once to his crew. But they could not move away fast enough to miss the sound of the splash which the corpse from the *Delight* made as it fell into the sea, and it might be that the *Pequod* received a "ghostly baptism" from the spray that arose. Nor did they get away so fast that the crew of the *Delight* did not see the strange lifebuoy that the *Pequod*'s carpenter had made of Queequeg's unused coffin.[2] A voice followed them as the two ships moved away from each other:

> "In vain, oh, ye strangers, ye fly our sad burial; ye but turn us your taffrail to show us your coffin."

With the gams of the *Bachelor* and the *Rachel* Ahab had refused to acknowledge the existence of joy and sorrow in life as his obsession overwhelmed him. It had not been entirely easy for him to allow the *Bachelor* to sail out of his life, but he had no intention of allowing the *Pequod* to delay for a gam.

---

[2] Queequeg had once fallen so ill that his death seemed certain and a coffin was made according to his specifications. He recovered, however, and the coffin was made into a lifebuoy. See Chapters CX and CXXVI.

Moreover, even though he could acknowledge Captain Gardiner's distress, he could also harden his heart and refuse to help the beseeching father. But here with the *Delight*, he cannot not avoid his baptism of death, the ghostly spray which repeats the theme of his baptizing of the harpoon with which he hoped to bring about the death of Moby Dick and achieve his revenge—"*Ego non baptizo te in nomine patris, sed in nomine diaboli.*"

The meeting with the *Delight* has some of the qualities of the meeting with the *Albatross*—the first and last gams find us at the same point on our voyage "round the world," that outward limit of circumnavigation. We have that same impression of the stark whiteness of bleached wood which characterized the *Albatross*. Upon the *Albatross* sailed an apathetic, despairing captain and his forlorn crew, evidently weighed down by some unnamed burden. So upon the *Delight* sailed a hollow-cheeked, grieving captain and his men, who are preoccupied with the grisly work of death.

As the *Pequod* comes to the end of its voyage we remember the words of Father Mapple. The symbolic appearance of the *Delight* had been prefigured in the sermon which he addressed to the sailors who gathered in his church before they left on their perilous journey:

> "But oh! shipmates! on the starboard hand of every woe, there is a sure delight, and higher the top of that delight, than the bottom of the woe is deep. . . .Delight is to him, whom all the waves of the billows of the seas of the boisterous mob can never shake from this sure Keel of the Ages. And eternal delight and deliciousness will be his, who coming to lay him down, can say with his final breath—O Father! . . .I have striven to be Thine, more than to be this world's, or mine own. . . .I leave eternity to Thee. . . . "

Therefore, in spite of its forlorn aspect, the *Delight*, for the stern believer, held out hope that "delight" would be attained in the hereafter, as Melville implies in *Clarel*:

> Even death may prove unreal at the last,
> And stoics be astounded into heaven.

How ironic is Fate—as ironic as the appearance of the last ship the *Pequod* was to meet! Here Ahab has sailed round the world and has reached the Japanese Sea, thousands of miles from Nantucket. He has given up all his humanity for his "delight," perhaps not the delight Father Mapple extolled, but the burning hope of delight in the attainment of an ideal enshrined in his flint-like heart. Yet questioning whether such ideals will ever be realized, Melville warns, no matter how far we may roam in search of our elusive dream, we must be prepared for disillusionment, even failure:

> Round the world! There is much in that sound to inspire proud feelings; but whereto does all that circumnavigation conduct? Only through numberless perils to the very point whence we started, where those that we left behind secure, were all the time before us.

The demon phantom that had beckoned Ahab in his long voyage had now brought him to the brink of his final battle. Only one chink showed in his armor: his fearful foreboding of death as he strove to escape sight and sound of the burial on board the *Delight*. Fear and doubt seemed to rise in him as a result of his meeting with the mourning ship, and later on, in "The Symphony," he reveals much of his thought to Starbuck. But, characteristically, his dread leads him to think of himself, Ahab, not of the men around him who may share his tragic end. He thinks of Ahab wandering, Ahab deprived,

Ahab in the grip of a furious mania, Ahab friendless, perhaps dead—these were the preoccupations of his self-pity.

For some short moments even Ahab seems to understand that other humans do exist and that he is friendless. One magnanimous thought breaks through, as when he speaks with Starbuck he remembers that his first mate has a wife and child at home in Nantucket who represent for him "top-gallant delight." Telling him not to lower for Moby Dick when the chase begins, Ahab exclaims, "Stay on board . . .lower not when I do. . . .That hazard shall not be thine!"

But loyal Starbuck, too, is lost when the *Pequod* is finally brought to its death by Moby Dick. Not even Queequeg's coffin would save him, as it would save Ishmael.

With the departure of the *Delight* the social encounters of the *Pequod* come to an end and the fatal chase for Moby Dick begins in reality. Ahab, who throughout the voyage had never made a forthright attempt to communicate with his fellow man, is destroyed by the very quest for which he denied his kinship with those who followed him. Sharing his destruction are the men whose loyalty he commands and whose humanity he rejects. They were merely "manufactured" or "mechanical" men whom he treated as tools by which he hoped to accomplish his purpose. Only one of the *Pequod*'s crew survives, Ishmael "the wanderer," an enigmatic figure who has never given whole-hearted loyalty to Ahab but who has remained somewhat aloof—a figure who may represent Melville's *alter ego*. After having suffered agonizing loneliness as a solitary survivor floating upon a deserted sea, Ishmael is at last rescued by the *Rachel*, who persists in the search for her "children," the same ship that had been denied help by Ahab. Ironically, the "child" she rescued was not hers, for he belonged to Ahab's *Pequod*. In the final reckoning evil is not returned for evil, but good is given in spite of the evil which has been done, even though the good is not commensurate with the evil which Ahab has wrought.

The *Rachel*, symbol of never-failing, all-encompassing love, finally brings the saving grace without which there would be no hope for humanity, a grace which contradicts the despair of the *Delight*. Her action in saving life instead of allowing it to be destroyed, is in contrast to the usual spirit of the gams which suggest the need for a different approach to human relations. Obviously the approach displayed by the *Pequod* leads only to negative consequences—inexorably to the ultimate in negation: annihilation.

12

The Gams of *Moby-Dick* as Reflections of Society

Gradual alienation from the society in which he lived was a salient feature of Herman Melville's life and thought. His writings, therefore, reflect varying states of mind concerning the worth of the values held dear by most of his contemporaries in the rapidly industrializing America of which he was proud but at the same time critical. Spiritually he was so intimately involved in society's concerns that he directed his enormous intellectual energies toward them to the exclusion of almost everything else. The contemplation of society and the plight of the individual enmeshed in society's web absorbed him to such an extent that through his writings he persistently sought to diagnose the causes of the human dilemma and, if possible, to work out solutions—at least on the level of the individual.

Early in his life Melville came into unpleasant contact with the swirling forces of a fast-changing society. Transitions in the spheres of economic power caused the financial ruin of his family, which led to his father's premature death when Melville was twelve years old. Thus his early manhood was spent in poverty and humiliation, which was at the root of a bitterness sharpened later on by the sight of others' miseries brought about by the inexorable economic changes which were transforming the American landscape. More ominously, they were transforming the American character as well in a direction which seemed to Melville sinister, for he saw no compensating benefit to the ordinary individual to be derived from these vaunted changes.

Economic necessity was the chief motivation which led the young Melville to sign aboard a merchantman as a common seaman, starting him on a career lasting several years. As a result, he did not receive the advanced schooling which many contemporary American writers enjoyed, but reading was a lifelong source of education for him.[1] His viewpoint was widened, too, by voyages to England, South America, and the South Seas, where he came into contact with diverse cultures, and these experiences served as a spiritual awakening through which his thought blossomed.

As a result of his experiences with primitive cultures Melville became fascinated with probing into the wellsprings of human life before, he assumed, it became tainted with civilization. He had thought that by observing a purer and more innocent way of life, perhaps he could isolate the unwholesome factors which served to make life in civilization so patently unfulfilling. The observations gleaned from these years provided him with the concepts of cultural relativism

---

[1] For an overview of the books he preferred see Willard Thorp's introduction to *Herman Melville: Representative Selections* (New York: American Book Company, 1938), xxiv-xxviii. Also helpful is Merton M. Sealts' *Melville's Reading* (Columbia: University of South Carolina Press, 1988).

which broadened his understanding of humanity's evolution, but he was disillusioned, also. Among the supposedly benign, untainted cultures he discovered to his horror that cannibalism was still being practiced. Having become aware of the falsity lying beneath the general perception of these primitive cultures Melville anticipated Freud, who expressed some gentle skepticism on the subject of true happiness in such supposedly innocent societies.

On the other hand, such experiences as witnessing unimaginable wretchedness in crowded industrial cities posed a dilemma for Melville. Could primitive societies be seen as closer to man's natural character? Or had man progressed in virtue as he had evolved from primitivism? If so, why the abuses of modern life—the poverty, misery, even degradation of people in the most highly advanced cultures? And why the callousness of those who held wealth and power? What really was civilization?

Characteristically, he did not give way to black despair. His Calvinist upbringing could have provided him with strength to withstand such emotional shocks. A Calvinist should not feel too much surprise at unregenerate man's propensity toward evil, though he may recoil at its actual proof. Moreover, Melville could not help being affected by the sturdy American pragmatism then in the air, which declares that there must be a rational (or scientific) solution for every problem.

Melville's seafaring-related sojourns in England influenced him emotionally and intellectually even more than his South Seas adventures, since that country exhibited the same tendencies as his own America; in fact, England had proceeded even farther along the relentless path to industrialization, having been its pioneer. Some of the stark truths of the industrial world were revealed to him in Liverpool, where he witnessed the plight of the poor, some of them homeless, friendless, suffering people without hope. Such sights formed the basis of a novel, *Redburn: His First Voyage* (1849), and created in him a permanent empathy with the destitute and downtrodden, especially those whom industrial society had rejected as unfit.[2] One of the most devastating of the scenes he witnessed was that of a young woman huddled beneath a grating in a busy street in Liverpool. She was clutching a baby to her, and apparently both were dying of exposure and starvation while her fellow human beings bustled by, unaware or uncaring.

In spite of the disillusion which some of these experiences brought, they also awoke in Melville a tolerance which allowed him to encompass all varieties of belief (and unbelief) within his thought and, as a result, his writings are marked by a unique understanding which set him apart from most of his countrymen. Only Melville could have portrayed such incisive characters as the crew of the *Pequod*. Who but Melville could have created Queequeg and made him endearing in spite of his heathenish ways?

Upon Melville's return from his ocean adventures, the problems of his own society continued to haunt him. He had reason to be resentful of the forerunners and beneficiaries of

---

[2] Justification for the criteria by which they were judged would find a perfect rationale in social Darwinism. See Richard Hofstader, *Social Darwinism in American Thought, 1860-1915* (Philadelphia: University of Philadelphia Press, 1945).

the social changes of the times, the rising economic class which had caused financial ruin and psychological wounds within his family. Another source of bitterness for Melville was the fact that he could not adequately provide for his family by his writings and was often in debt to his father-in-law, whose social philosophy he opposed.[3] He came to believe, finally, that the greatest contributing factor to the burden of human misery was the unique character of modern civilization. Since the artificial values of contemporary society were contrary to man's natural essence, he reflected, their eradication would be beneficial to humanity as a whole. These artificial values included a veritable worship of money: never did Melville forget the role that avarice and greed play in shaping men's character and destiny, a theme which would appear again and again in his writings. The scourge of an inscrutable, powerful, alienated society which was impressed upon Melville's consciousness at an early age gave him an understanding of the helplessness of the individual who struggles against forces which are beyond his control— yet who must come to terms with them somehow or lose touch with reality.

As part of his broad vision of the human condition, Melville acknowledged the indispensable contribution made by whalemen from all places of the earth as they labored and often died on their long and risky voyages to bring indispen-

---

[3] His father-in-law was Chief Justice Lemuel Shaw of the Massachusetts Supreme Court. Slavery was the main issue which divided Melville and Shaw. But only through a loan from his father-in-law was Melville able to purchase his farm near Pittsfield in the Berkshires. Justice Shaw also gave him money for his long-desired trip to the Middle East.

sable resources to those who stayed on land. The men shown in *Moby-Dick* were different from "landlubbers."[4] Members of a whaler's complement came from islands all over the world, the men being picked up at their home islands by the outbound ships and dropped off again on the homeward voyage. In spite of his unusual broad-mindedness, however, Melville shared part of the traditional *ethos* of his culture. As an example of this, he saw the men engaged in the American whaling industry neatly divided into those who furnished the "brains" (the white people—here identified as the "native Americans") and those who diligently and willingly provided the "brawn" (all other people), as explained in "Knights and Squires" in *Moby-Dick*:

> Not one in two of the many thousand men before the mast employed in the American whale fishery, are Americans born, though pretty nearly all the officers are; . . . the native Americans liberally provide the brains; the rest of the world as generously supplying the muscles.

Denoting Anglo-Americans as "native Americans" is another of the notions that demonstrate how much a child of his century he was, when North American Indians were thought to be "foreign" in their own land, and African-Americans were not thought to be "Americans born," even though America was the land of their birth! These denotations relating to the world's peoples, noticeable even in Melville, underline the narrowness of the thought of his American contemporaries. When he tried to break away from this eth-

---

[4] See Chapter XL, "Midnight, Forecastle," for an example of the many nationalities represented by the *Pequod's* crew.

nocentrism, he lost some of his popularity, for not everyone could go as far as to admit that other cultures had moral traditions comparable to those of the Western world.

Yet we should not construe this passage to mean that Melville thought the non-Americans inferior, for his ideal of democracy included a great respect for the "brawn," a concept which did not, strictly speaking, accommodate itself well to the disdainful thought of the expanding American *bourgeoisie*, of which Melville was an uneasy member. In his eulogy to the "august dignity" of the working man he exclaims,

> Thou shalt see it shining in the arm that wields a pick or drives a spike; that democratic dignity which, on all hands, radiates without end from God Himself!

Since in the United States an enormous number of non-Americans worked with picks and drove spikes to build the railways and canals, for example, it must be that he made no distinction between white and colored as far as "democratic dignity" was concerned. Seen from the vantage point of our times Melville might appear to be unduly imbued with pride of race, but it is to him that we owe many insights which have led to greater understanding between peoples. Much of his pride in the Anglo-Saxon culture was based upon his belief that democracy, which could hold promise for everyone, had its roots and would see its future in this culture.

Melville had grown to adulthood with a firm belief in the ideals of democracy. He felt, as did many of his countrymen, that the future of the world lay with the viability of the American nation. Paradoxically, however, the characteristic manifestations of this new age—a burgeoning and greedy industrialism coupled with a brutal, anachronistic slavery on the American plantations—denigrated the value of the person, and thus were the antithesis of democratic ideals. Moreover, in *Mardi*, published in 1849, the year of the California gold rush, Melville had already expressed the opinion that America was not necessarily bound for Utopia, that what was considered progress was not necessarily leading to social betterment.[5]

In *Mardi* Melville reminded his readers of the shortsightedness of their rush to reject spiritual values, thus foreshadowing *Moby-Dick* with its more explicit warnings against the pursuit of chimerical goals. *Mardi* contains the words of the seer who wrote the "anonymous scrolls":

> Time is made up of various ages; and each thinks its own a novelty. But embedded in the walls of the pyramids, which outrun all chronologies, sculptured stones are found, belonging to yet older fabrics. And as in the mound-building period of yore, so every age thinks its erections will endure forever. . . .

> Throughout all eternity, the parts of the past are but parts of the future reversed. In the old footprints, up and down, you mortals go, eternally travelling your Sierras. And not more infallible the ponderings of the Calculating Machine than the deductions from the decimals of history.

The mental and physical hardships which characterized Melville's first twenty-five years provided him with a spiritual ore from which he was to cut many rare gems, but the

---

[5] For an analysis of *Moby-Dick* as political allegory see Willie T. Weathers, "Melville and the Nineteenth Century Scene" (University of Texas Studies in Literature and Language, Vol. I). Also Alan Heimert in "*Moby-Dick* and American Political Symbolism" (*American Quarterly* 15, Winter, 1963) takes a close look at the actual contemporary political scene.

rarest of these did not appear until he had published *Moby-Dick* in 1851. Yet it was not well-received when it appeared, for in the opinion of many readers he seemed to espouse an un-Christian moral anarchy. His earlier works had been popular because of their fairly straightforward adventure themes, but in *Moby-Dick* Melville had moved away from his contemporaries. The antipathy some critics showed towards this novel had a profound effect upon him, which he could not always conceal. He made a wry, but also bitter, comment to his good friend Nathaniel Hawthorne, who was also concerned with the darker side of life, that among his readers he was known only as the man who had lived among cannibals. He felt that the prodigious amount of creative energy he had spent upon the writing of *Moby-Dick* would never be entirely recovered.

Perhaps Melville's reading public could not be blamed for their confusion in regard to his seemingly new stance. Although *Moby-Dick* would someday come to be looked upon as his masterpiece—even the greatest American novel—at that time when the American spirit of expansion and enterprise was at its height, *Moby-Dick* seemed to deny the rightness of society's goals.

Ahab has been described glowingly as "the American cultural hero, the image of the American of his time, captain of industry and of his soul, exploiter of nature, good, progressive American."[6] Melville himself considered his whaling adventures intensely educational, calling them his "Harvard

---

[6] Richard Chase, *Herman Melville, a Critical Study* (New York: Macmillan, 1949), 43-44.

and Yale." But Melville made it clear that Ahab's course was not the one which led to happiness or fulfillment. If we accept this interpretation of Ahab as the cultural hero, we shall be able to read into his contacts with others, as pictured graphically in the gams of the *Pequod*, his creator's dissatisfaction with such a "hero." It could be argued that he implied that those who chose this as the heroic way were morbidly obsessed or insane, like Ahab. Ahab himself felt that his "demoniac" obsession was a form of madness. In "Sunset" he soliloquizes, "They think me mad—Starbuck does—but I'm demoniac, I am madness maddened!"[7]

The Albatross and the Delight: Society Gone Awry

Moby-Dick carries on *Mardi*'s theme of the fruitless quest, but enhances it with other pertinent ones such as the alienation of the individual in a society which was becoming increasingly attuned to the values and pace required by the machine. The gams can be seen as parables of Melville's attitude toward his contemporaries who were defined by their allegiance to social goals antithetical to the development of the intrinsic nobility of humanity's heart and mind (at least in their potential).

The gams of the *Albatross* and the *Delight*, which form the first and the last meetings of the *Pequod*, emphasize symbolically the dehumanizing effect of society's course of action and, moreover, its futility. "Round the world" we sail on this

---

[7] It is significant that Ahab mentions Starbuck. The first mate would not have dared tell Ahab that he was mad, but in Starbuck's eyes (the "magic glass") Ahab could see that he thought so, and evidently Starbuck's opinion matters to Ahab, much as he would like to deny it.

voyage—to what? Knowledge, control over nature, material luxury, political or personal power? And yet we find ourselves in the same position, faced with evil, despair, and suffering on a personal level, social injustice on a national level, and war on the international level. Perhaps Melville was pointing out to his contemporaries that this discouraging outcome of their quest might be the starting-point for a re-examination of their conduct in each human relationship, since their chosen course had brought so little happiness and harmony to society. The so-called benefits of materialism, he feared, would ultimately lead to results much worse than the original state from which people were frantically trying to escape as they strove for material possessions and power.

One of the results of this constant quest for power and material plenty, Melville believed, would be ultimate subservience to the mechanical processes which man had devised to nullify his own weakness in the effort to "subdue" Nature for his own purposes. But this release from physical labor for some resulted in slavery of various kinds for others, Melville observed. As an example, the gradual loss of humanity in factory workers was described in his short story, "The Tartarus of Maids" (1855), which grew out of his observation of women at work in a paper mill: human beings were supposed to be freed from exhausting toil by means of machinery, but instead they themselves had become its captives.[8]

---

[8] Carolyn L. Karcher provides a detailed look at Melville's attitudes toward slavery in *Shadow over the Promised Land: Slavery, Race, and Violence in Melville's America* (Baton Rouge: Louisiana State Press, 1980).

Machinery—that vaunted slave of humanity—here stood menially served by human beings, who served mutely and cringingly as the slave serves the Sultan. The girls did not so much seem accessory wheels to the general machinery as mere cogs to the wheels.[9]

The pallid, apathetic girls whom he sees working at these machines correspond to the spiritless captain of the *Albatross*. By presenting this shadowy, depressing gam first, Melville strikes a note of prophecy in regard to American society. An ebullient Ahab is striking out on a new voyage, but his fate will be even worse than that of the crew of the *Albatross*. Here was a captain at the end of a voyage which had begun probably as cheerily as that of the *Pequod*. But Ahab has no time for reflection upon this. Could Melville be trying to sound a warning that the direction America was taking as it began its new voyage into the complete industrialization of society could have effects upon humanity which would become more ominous with the passage of time unless humanitarian efforts were made? This theme was echoed later by such thinkers as Lewis Mumford who in the 1950's, the time of swelling consumerism after World War II, observed that modern people were separated from reality by the welter of material goods which surrounded them to such an extent that they could be described as living in "a ghost-world." [10]

---

[9] Melville saw this system benefiting some but taking liberty away from others. Nicolai Berdiaev observes in *The Fate of Man in the Modern World* (Ann Arbor: University of Michigan Press, 1961; 1935) that one of the dilemmas of free societies is that liberty has become a paradox: in general it has come to protect the rights of the privileged few and a defender of capitalists—which phenomenon is attributed to the overweening power of money. Berdaiev was one of the principal exponents of Christian existentialism.

[10] Lewis Mumford, *Art and Technics* (New York: Columbia University Press, 1952),

The *Albatross* manifested this quality of ghostliness with the grayish white of its appearance and its supernatural silence. Each man aboard, especially the captain, gave the impression that he has indeed lost touch with reality.

Since there is no human interchange between these two ships, Melville may be considering the role of Nature as it relates to humanity, or *vice versa*, as we are invited to consider it, too. What wrong had the captain of the *Albatross* committed? Was it wrong for him to kill whales; was the enterprise of whaling an offense against Nature? The purpose for which they were killed, perhaps, can be compared to the killing of the buffalo and the elephant in this same era. Whales were useful to mankind, that is all. Whaling was an economic enterprise to benefit society. But Nature was not being replenished by man as he carried out the cruel pursuit of the whale for its oil, nor did anyone think it necessary to do so.

The American whaling industry during its peak provided most of the world's needs for oil. As soon as a better source of industrial oil, petroleum, was found, however, the world was inclined to forget the sacrifices of whales and whalemen. The whale has been credited with having unknowingly benefited mankind by furnishing the civilized world with the privileges of light, perfume, and food, but this is a human-centered notion. The whales had no choice while they were needed: they were cruelly and coldly marked for suffering and death. Gradually, if reckless use continued, Nature's plenty could be diminished almost to extinction, and people

97f.

in the future might become penitents, even as the Ancient Mariner was, but no amount of penitence could enable them to avoid eventual retribution. Was it the burden of penitence that was weighing on the spirit of the captain of the *Albatross* for some unnamed iniquity? Melville does not explain.

In the light of economic realities, there might have been a further, more understandable reason for the dejection which haunted the *Albatross*. On a mundane plane, it might be that the captain of the *Albatross* was on his homeward course with an empty ship, the worst of all circumstances for a whaling captain and crew. Perhaps they had killed no whales at all and therefore were failures in the eyes of society—and in their own eyes. This might mean that the men would have to ship out again immediately, since they would have no money to sustain themselves over a resting period. Melville would see this as a form of slavery to an economic system which tolerated no human frailties. The clothing of the crews, "like the skins of beasts" denotes this—one could be shut out from society without money. Melville knew that well and never minimized its significance, its cost to the individual in humiliation and deprivation.

As for Ahab and his attitude toward Nature, it is the extremity of his contempt of it that is most noticeable. What Ahab lacks completely is empathy. Nor does he see himself as a trustee of Nature: Nature is there for him to exploit.[11] His desire for revenge has warped him, made him bitter and callous (except occasionally when he lapses into self-pity). In

---

[11]This, of course, was the prevailing thought of Melville's day, a corollary of the machine-age interpretation of Darwinism.

his obsession to kill the whale who has maimed him, Ahab anthropomorphizes Moby Dick, ascribes to him human-like intent, not the natural instinct of an animal which fights desperately for its life, as Starbuck would point out to Ahab. Before this, Ahab had sailed for understandable material gain, to make a hard-won living for himself and his family in Nantucket; now it is to assuage his rage, and even his family is forgotten.

The Town Ho—the Capitalist Society?

The gam of the *Town-Ho* is so complicated that sifting out the main themes is by no means easy. But since societal concerns were never far from Melville's mind and consequently pervaded all his writings, we may be justified in looking for social criticism here.[12] Harsh as it is in tone, this gam can be a reflection of how Melville saw the real world, the economic world, the political world, the world peopled by struggling human beings. It would be an oversimplification to say that the society aboard the *Town-Ho* represents the American free enterprise system manipulated by the "invisible hand" of *laissez faire* economics, but on board we find related chaotic, frenetic emotions, rebellion against rules, and treachery abundantly portrayed, just as they happen in an economic system where law does not rein in these passions. It was obvious that law had broken down on the *Town-Ho*.

---

[12]Willard Thorp writes of Melville's social consciousness, "Every serious book or article which Melville wrote is a variation on the social theme." In *Herman Melville*, xcviii.

In this gam we have two outstanding social themes which reflect Melville's indictment of American civilization, neither of which was designed to earn him any popularity, for these were related to the "gospel of wealth" by which most Americans lived —at least those who were profiting from the system as it existed.[13]

The first indictment was directed toward the capitalist social philosophy and its concomitant factory and plantation systems put in place and maintained by powerful men who felt little moral responsibility toward their workers and slaves. Not only that, Melville decided, these powerful men, sometimes euphemistically called "robber barons," jockeyed themselves into high position by amoral actions motivated by greed: they wasted their time and energy planning unscrupulous maneuvers in order to outwit their fellow moguls as well as any other creature whose money they could grab with impunity. The law was on their side because they could buy privilege and "justice." But they were also buying the souls of their workers, who lived in unconscionable poverty in spite of their toils. In the 1850's both industrial workers and plantation slaves were economic pawns in a system which made human beings subsidiary to the product of their labor, and both the Southern slave owner and the urban *entrepreneur* came in for their share of Melville's opprobrium. Under this dual system, human relationships suffered intolerable degradation.

---

[13]The gospel of wealth was an amalgam of concepts borrowed from Darwinism and Christianity.

Melville's second indictment against American society appears in "The *Town-Ho's* Story" as part of the conversation Ishmael had with a circle of Spanish friends in Lima, Peru. This forms the vehicle for his admonitions to the Christian churches and to its clergy. Christianity had begun as a religion to address and assuage the sufferings of the poor and the downtrodden, he reasoned. No matter what one's station in life, all were equal in the eyes of Heaven. Since the leaders of the churches which had grown out of this religious core had historically vowed to cherish every member of their faith, they certainly should not wish to stand by while the powerful abused the weak. This was unthinkable in a profoundly Christian society. Nevertheless, this is how it seemed to be, for the rich (even in spite of venality) seemed to be made more welcome "in the patronizing lee" of the church than the ordinary citizen who had only the proverbial mite to offer. Melville was bitter against an institution that would pay respect to blatant transgressors of the creed of Christianity to which they gave only lip service. He saw this as an unbearable hypocrisy. Even more, it smacked of moral corruption, if one really analyzed the situation with absolute clarity and without ulterior motives.

In the gam of the *Town-Ho* these two themes are echoed in the interlocking actions: the events on board emulate the situation in contemporary society, while Ishmael's visit in the Golden Inn carries Melville's criticism of that society. Contributing to the complexity of the gam, Ishmael is telling a tale of a previous episode on the *Town-Ho* before he shipped on the *Pequod*. The story is, of course, based upon hearsay— and how many years had elapsed since the disaster of the *Pequod* we do not know. But from Ishmael we become aware of a situation on the *Town-Ho* wherein Radney, the first mate, is a "capitalist," that is, he is part owner of the ship. Radney has few endearing qualities: he is overbearing and physically repulsive: therefore he is "ugly" in two senses. This is given importance in the conversation of the crewmen who are toiling at the pumps of the ship because it had sprung a serious leak (probably damaged by swordfish, they say). In this conversation the handsome seaman Steelkilt, noting that the first mate is within earshot, makes humorously sardonic comments about Radney's investment in the ship, declaring that the swordfish are "playing the devil with his estate."

It is significant that Steelkilt knows that Radney is listening, but he pretends not to be aware of him. Steelkilt is purposely baiting Radney, who is sensitive about his ugliness, saying that "old Rad," it is rumored, has a great deal of money invested in mirrors in which to preen himself. He wants to insult Radney without seeming to do so, and in this way tries slyly to undermine the crew's respect for the mate, as well as to fuel their resentment at his capitalist status while they commiserate about having to toil at the pumps—irrationally "Radney's pumps." Steelkilt can be seen as driven by a will-to-power as much as Radney is: he has ambitions to be the ringleader of a group of mutinously-inclined comrades. He seems to have an instinct for rebellion and the audacity to carry it out.

On his part, Radney pretends that he has not heard these biting remarks which make him a laughing-stock among the men. Instead, he approaches the men and roars at them to increase their pumping; his arrogance fuels in Steelkilt a desire for revenge, for the toilers are at the point of exhaustion.

Radney and Steelkilt are wearing "pasteboard masks," as Ahab calls such false appearances, unable to express their animosity except by a perverse communication.[14] When Steelkilt's stint at the pumps is over, he is exhausted and sits down to rest. But vengeful Radney orders him to sweep the decks and perform other menial tasks which are not part of his duties. This sets the stage for a violent, possibly fatal confrontation, which Melville senses was "pre-ordained."

Simmering beneath the men's actions in these seemingly ordinary events is the substance of the class struggle *in parvo*. One of Melville's anxieties for American society was that the discrepancy between the rich and poor, which seemed to be increasing, might lead workers and slaves to rebel against the abuses to which they were subjected and thus arouse them to the point where class warfare would tear society apart. Here it is quite obvious that the men do resent Radney for his enhanced status: he is both first mate and part owner of the ship in which they must toil for low wages. They resent having to do extra work at the pumps for the overbearing "plutocrat" Radney.

The resentment and lack of communication among the men lead to events which destroy the harmony and efficiency of the ship. The *Town-Ho*, representing society, is already damaged, which puts a greater strain on the lower classes of men to keep it afloat for capitalist gain, as they see it. It is not a sensible attitude, of course, because they would not be better off if the ship capsized. But Melville held no brief for

---

[14] Ahab believes that natural phenomena also wear these "pasteboard masks"

their rationality—they are swayed by their passions, as were the men of the *Jeroboam*.

The captain, who in this metaphor could represent governmental leadership, is rather a feckless fellow who is not sure of how to handle the problems which arise—his ultimate solution seems to be only to threaten with a pistol or two, but he never carries out his threat.[15] He is not in favor of Radney's violent frontal approach; nevertheless, he does not seem to be able to prevent his first mate from committing the rash act which puts murderous thoughts in Steelkilt's heart. But neither does he try to understand the actions of the men—and he is intimidated by their organizer, Steelkilt. Like Captain Mayhew of the *Jeroboam*, he is not an heroic figure. Even so, this captain is in a compromising position: Radney, being first mate and part owner of the ship, is both beneath him as his officer and above him as employer, which adds to the many ambiguities in this gam. What should be the proper attitude of the captain, who by all rules of the sea should be in complete command—"in lieu of land law"—but who must operate the ship according to his employer's wishes?

The ship is saved from complete disaster because Steelkilt's plan of murder was not carried out, since Radney met death when they lowered for Moby Dick. But this in no way changes the aggrieved Steelkilt from deciding to mutiny at the first opportunity. He takes matters into his own hands

---

[15]This parallel is appropriate, since in Melville's time, government was not expected to regulate. Public affairs fell into such chaos, however, that in the 1880's business and industry saw a need for regulations, but these were not designed with workers in mind. These advances had to wait for the rise of the trade unions.

once again and finally succeeds in his ambition to be the ringleader of a group of mutineers, while the captain eventually loses his authority over them and allows them to escape the justice which should have been meted out to them.

Melville shows us how weak are the props which sustain the Temple of Law, ostensibly built by Reason, a temple which can easily be undermined by a blind Samson in his fury.[16] And this Samson, as he implies, might be the uncontrollable power which man has loosed through his machines, or most likely a power unleashed in man himself because of the availability of that power for destructive ends.

No one comes out a winner throughout the unremitting conflicts which plague the *Town-Ho*: Radney does not live to enjoy his expected prosperity; the two Canallers, Steelkilt's betrayers, are flogged within an inch of their lives; the captain captures no whales, even though they had had Moby Dick on a line; the *Town-Ho* continues to be plagued with leaks until it is disabled and must be repaired; Steelkilt mutinies successfully but can never rejoin the American whaling fleet for fear of retribution; the men who stay with the *Town-Ho* are worked almost to death trying to get the ship back into sailing condition, while the captain must settle for less qualified Tahitans to replace the skilled mutineers.

The many layers of complexities in this gam include the theme of corruption, symbolized by the locale in which Ishmael tells the sordid tale of the disabled ship. The city of Lima, Ishmael's friends tell him, is a metaphor for corruption,

---

[16]This metaphor is based on the story found in *Judges*, chapter 16, of the Old Testament.

even though the city is filled with churches—they are "more plentiful than billiard-tables" and "always open." Within the story are sprinkled oblique criticisms of the predominantly Protestant religion in America, oblique because they seem to be directed at the medieval Spanish Catholic Church. Ishmael's listeners exclaim that his remarks would be considered heretical by any friar or priest lurking nearby; therefore they jest that if he had lived during the Inquisition, he would have been subject to an *auto-da-fé*—and they warn him to get out of the moonlight so that he won't be seen.[17] These criticisms should not be made in broad daylight, Melville knew that well: here Ishmael has to avoid the moonlight, too! In effect, the book *Moby-Dick* was the bright "moonlight" in which Melville presented his views, heedless of the nineteenth century American version of the *auto-da-fé*.

Such passages as the following illustrate Melville's disapproval of organized religion and, by extension, his skepticism about the moral integrity of what he considered to be its smug clergy. In this instance Ishmael is speaking, describing for his curious listeners the lusty, frontier-like yet sanctimonious culture which had grown up in the vicinity of the Erie Canal, opened in 1827:

> ". . .Through all the wide contrasting scenery of those noble Mohawk countries, and especially, by rows of snow-white chapels, whose spires stand almost like milestones, flows one continual stream of Venetianly corrupt and often lawless life. There's your true Ashantee, gentlemen; there howl your pagans; where you ever find them, next door to you; under the long-flung shadow, and the

---

[17] An *auto-da-fé* was a cruel punishment inflicted upon condemned heretics during the Spanish Inquisition, which was in effect until 1820.

snug patronizing lee of churches. For by some curious fatality, as it is often noted of your metropolitan freebooters that they ever encamp around the halls of justice, so sinners, gentlemen, most abound in holiest vicinities."

Don Sebastian immediately asks, again in jest, "Is that a friar passing?" as if some suspicious friar could overhear such blasphemous comments and would come to the Inn to denounce Ishmael. No harm came to him, however, even from the "archiepiscopacy," but his story did come to an abrupt conclusion after he had sworn to its veracity—but only conditionally.

We assume that Melville is bringing the churches of his time to task for not exerting their influence to change society for the better according to Christian principles: instead of siding with the people, they were on the side of the plutocrats. In real life, however, this voice of Melville in *Moby-Dick* earned for him condemnation from the devout for his irreverence: he touched upon subjects, it was said, that should not be broached in such an ungentlemanly fashion.[18]

The Jeroboam: Demagogues and Desperation

The gams of the *Town-Ho* and the *Jeroboam* are loosely tied together by the figure of the fanatic Gabriel (whose fame has preceded him). Together they serve as vehicles for Melville's protests against the economic, political, and religious aspects of society. The gam of the *Jeroboam* can be construed as a prophecy related to the plight of society's masses crushed

---

[18]How could they forgive that scurrilous passage where Ishmael, resigning himself to sharing a bed at the crowded Spouter Inn with Queequeg, decided, "Better sleep with a sober cannibal than a drunken Christian!"

and demoralized by the contemporary irrational industrial system which has deprived them of their own volition. Falling back into superstition, the crew of the *Jeroboam* had become prey to a false prophet who held out hope of a celestial utopia.[19] Reason, symbolized by the *Jeroboam's* captain, was impotent against the irrational, demonic force personified by "Gabriel."

In spite of the persuasive arguments of political demagogues, as Melville might see it, the more America progressed along its present course, the farther away it would move from true democracy based upon reason. With reason undermined, society could regress to a level where the life of mankind would again be steeped in fear, barbarism, and superstition (as it did in the twentieth century with the advent of Adolf Hitler).[20] Here Melville is concerned with the seductive irrationality of the machine and the retrogressive influence of irrational religions. One might think that the factory system was the ultimate in rationality, but Melville did not see it that way, for his thought was not with the machine itself, but with the people who by some alchemy seemed to become part of it.[21] He felt that workers and slaves were being forced into molds which bore no relevance to

[19]These unfortunates bring to mind the ignorant masses as depicted in George Orwell's *1984*.

[20]Yet this irrational response to fear could be evidence that thereby the masses were asserting their humanity, albeit in a bizarre way—that at least their emotions were not atrophied yet and they were not entirely reduced to robots or androids.

[21]This process was illustrated with humor by Charles Chaplin in his motion picture, *Modern Times* (1936), a satire of mechanical civilization and how it affects the worker.

humane values, according to which human beings ought to be free to choose to live a noble existence based upon reason.

On the *Jeroboam* chaos had progressed to the point where a contagion threatened the health of the entire society, and it appeared that no one knew how to cure it. It is obvious that unorthodox religion, like the orthodox, offered no solution. In fact, it added to the problem by preaching, as zealot Gabriel did, that reason had no place in human life: he was ready to rid the ship of its true authority, the captain, by forcing him off the ship. Yet the falling away from the ways of reason rewarded the men with nothing but incipient madness and the plague which threatened the whole ship with death. On the *Jeroboam* we see a totalitarian state run by a fanatical autocrat. His religious passion is not directed toward the betterment of the society which swears allegiance to him, but toward the consolidation of his own powers.

This was not the message Americans wanted to hear, for they preferred to ally themselves with the social and economic goals proposed for them by those who, ironically, had most to gain from their misguided loyalty. Melville was pilloried for his stand on religion, but it was not his wish to destroy Christianity; it was his intention to give a strong reminder to its adherents, especially those high in the hierarchy, that they were being false to their calling. Because religion was such an integral part of American life in his era, Melville felt that the clergy must be reachable, since they were already dedicated to humanitarian endeavors, as they averred. His message, however, would have been too intimidating for those who had vested interests, financial or personal, in the perpetuation of the system as it was. As it appeared to him the churches were overly interested in collecting funds for missionaries to go into "benighted" societies to favor them with the blessings of Western civilization: Melville was candid about the futility of this enterprise. Very likely he would have seen modern efforts to bring all cultures up to Western standards of technology equally futile and destructive.

Most Americans in Melville's day felt that religion was the indispensable underpinning of society. At the same time they viewed the contemporary social organization as a given which should be inviolable; Melville, with a more visionary approach, saw society as humanity's creation which could be changed for the good of all, reasonably and with good will. For his argument he reached back to the era of the Declaration of Independence, but the good *bourgeoisie* shuddered to think that the masses would have the right to overthrow the government as their ancestors had done when it seemed inimical to the people's welfare: this dislocation certainly would not be good for business.

Although Melville wished to see changes in the society, he realized that people needed external constraints to prevent such disasters as occurred on the symbolic *Town-Ho*. The societies shown in the gams of the *Town-Ho* and the *Jeroboam*, unfortunately, lack the intelligent leadership to organize a way out of their difficulties by either revolution or mediation. Both the *Town-Ho* and the *Jeroboam* have captains who do not whole-heartedly accept the responsibilities of their position, and this defection brings in its train calamitous consequences for the ship's entire company. Captain Mayhew allows Gabriel, the manifestation of irrationality, to take command. The *Town-Ho*'s captain's valor is in question: Melville sarcastically calls him "valiant" when he is trying to quell a riot on board without getting too close to the fray—he tells his officers to take charge and sends his steward for his pistols, which he seems to have no intention of using. Steelkilt realizes this and becomes even bolder in his defiance of the captain's commands, just as Gabriel was emboldened by his captain's ineptitude. All members of the two crews seemed "pre-destinated" to contribute to the downfall of their ships' society, these microcosms of civilization. Is this perverseness part of human nature? At times Melville seems to believe so.

Three Gams as Mirrors of Ethnocentrism

Turning to American thought in its international aspects, we find that the gams of the *Jungfrau*, *Bouton de Rose*, and *Samuel Enderby* are instructive as reflections of certain attitudes which prevailed in Melville's time among the general population. The "Yankees" on board the *Pequod*, of whom Melville is essentially proud, assume matter-of-fact attitudes which seem to function well enough on the everyday plane of social relationships. We cannot criticize them in their dealings with the ungrateful Captain Derick of the *Jungfrau*, nor is there really any blame to be found with Stubb for his perfectly legal conduct toward the *Bouton de Rose*, since he, judged as a practical man, did them a favor by relieving the crew of their unsavory task. The actions in each case suited the situation. Any appeal to a higher principle than expediency is lacking; the Mosaic dictum, "an eye for an eye, a tooth for a tooth," suffices with the German ship, and legalistic reasoning exonerates Stubb in his dealings with the French.

Melville's thought rarely remained at the pragmatic level: — the twentieth century's situational ethics would never serve as a touchstone for his analysis. He constantly sought a way to integrate the complexities and ambiguities inherent in baffling social problems with an enlightened morality. By his derogatory remarks concerning legalism as a suitable rationale upon which to base one's actions (in "Fast Fish and Loose Fish") he suggests that it would be better to seek unifying principles to which men could appeal for guidance. These principles would be based upon the acceptance of moral responsibility in all relationships, for one cannot truly escape commitments to others by a mean adherence to a code which is based essentially on injustice and selfish expediency.

The international implications inherent in the drama of the *Jungfrau* can bear exploring. Her relations with the *Pequod* are fraught with anarchy, just as was the contemporary state of affairs between nations, when treaties merely organized the interludes between wars. In "Fast-Fish and Loose-Fish" Melville asks as he surveys this anarchy, "What was Poland to the Czar? What Greece to the Turk? what India to England? What at last will Mexico be to the United States? All Loose-Fish"[22]

In 1850 there was no unified Germany as it came to be known in the 1870's, a powerful militaristic state, which after its defeat of France had to be reckoned with as a world power. When the *Jungfrau* sailed the seas, its home harbor, Bremen, could claim only the prestige of being a port city for international trade in a confederation of states of mediocre status

---

[22]The guiding principles of the United Nations are comparable in concept as most nations agree that the extreme nationalism of the past had led only to reckless adventures. The great globe could not much longer be treated as a "loose fish" if the planet were to survive.

geopolitically. Therefore, the incongruous position the *Jung-frau* was in, not having oil enough to light her lamps, could be a subject of ridicule for the men on the *Pequod* —possibly as a reflection of Germany's lesser status. The nonchalant "Yan-kees" especially were proud of their high standing in the world of whaling, in spite of their being called "sea peasants" by British whalemen.

In the mid-century this lack of esteem was a source of resentment for ambitious Germans (notably those from Prus-sia), who were therefore willing to follow Bismarck's lead in changing the situation when the time was ripe.[23] It was not apparent in Melville's time that Germany's ardent resolve to occupy a preeminent place among the nations would lead her into the development of technologies that would dazzle and dismay the world. He could not have known that the German people, immersed in this technological world, would de-velop machine age characteristics which would give them a world-wide reputation for a kind of robotization: "good Ger-man order" became a watchword for rationality, but the Ger-man nation's ultimate destiny was to be chauvinistic irrationality under a supremely amoral and irrational *Führer*.[24] If he had known, Melville would not have been surprised: this is just what he surmised would happen if people gave their souls to the machine.

[23]In 1870-71 Germany began her international career by victory in the Franco-Prussian War.

[24]Hitler's aims were to be achieved by a "military machine," his armed forces.

Melville proposes to illustrate the anarchy which characterizes social relationships in another way. This, too, is done entertainingly, but no less seriously, in the gam of the *Bouton de Rose*. Although his foremost social concern was the waste and misuse of human beings in a commercial, technological (and militaristic) society, he was also ahead of most of his generation in seeing that the counterpart of industrial exploitation was a similar reckless attitude toward Nature on the part of both the industrialists and the frontiersmen, whether they were cattle barons, lumber kings or intrepid homesteaders. Nor were plantation owners above reproach. Cotton-growing, which led to soil depletion, continually demanded new land, which was exploited in the same manner as the old. Cotton, however, was needed to feed the expanding textile mills., not only in the United States, but also abroad. Britain, for example was one of America's best customers for this industry. The gam of the *Rose Bud* brings out the wasteful uses of natural resources in that it illustrates the profligate use of whales as being unavoidable under existing conditions, but deplorable all the same.

In the United States economic and social conditions were revealing the inner logic of the industrialization which was gathering ineluctable momentum in Melville's century, a logic which he perceived more clearly than most. There was no way for Melville to predict the future proportions of the waste and misuse of natural resources as the westward migration through the American continent took its toll of forest, plain, and wild life, but in his metaphor of the great globe itself as a loose fish he expressed the idea that there was a kind of moral anarchy implicit in the habits which mankind tended to develop in the use of its planetary home. If one had wounded a whale without capturing it, as it floated on the sea it became fair game for anyone, just as it did when Stubb made his shrewd discovery of the ambergris. In the chapter, "Does the Whale's Magnitude Diminish?—Will He Perish?" Melville marshals several arguments against the likelihood of the extinction of whales, for he felt, or hoped, that they had the patina of immortality, in contrast to the buffalo and the elephant. Perhaps inwardly he knew that this was merely wishful thinking, for he minced no words when he so graphically described the slaughter of whales, rather bitterly reflecting that the world cared little. [25]

The days when nations could enjoy the luxury of seizing "loose fish" are gone, but the attitudes remain. When Melville asks, "What is the great globe itself but a Loose Fish?" we are reminded of the often irreversible onslaughts already made upon the global environment by technological exploitation— the thinning ozone layer, smog from industry and automobiles, polluted seas, depleted forests, acid rain, the decimation of plant and animal species (including whales), and other disasters which confront the world.[26] Moreover, within the concept of the "great globe" as a "loose fish" modern people can read implications for space war., something which not even Melville could have imagined, yet space stations could presumably capture a "loose fish" world.

---

[25] Yet among the crews there were some who tried to mitigate the whales' "piteous" suffering during a chase: Starbuck, for example, reproved Flask for his cruelty when they were bringing in the whale which they won from the *Jungfrau*.

[26] In *Israel Potter* Melville notes that even then the Thames River was polluted by "vicinity to man" and looked like "one murky sheet of sewage."

In the final analysis, the *Pequod* actually had derived the most material benefits from her encounters with the French and German whalers: she brought in the old whale which the two ships had fought over, and Stubb found his hoard of ambergris. Nevertheless, the deceived *Bouton de Rose* thought she had benefited and was satisfied; the *Jungfrau* left the scene as empty-handed as she had come, but she had influenced events in spite of it, and this is significant. Perhaps the *Pequod*'s success in obtaining most of the benefits was symbolic of America's growing richness, for she was drawing wealth to herself from all sources, domestic and international. Yet in that very wealth lay a danger, Melville believed.

For Melville the appalling perversions of social values most destructive to the nation's integrity stemmed from greed: in its train came the host of abuses with which he was constantly concerned. The fact that the powerful in society could ignore the rights of the weak with impunity in a democracy angered him, as he exclaimed, "What are the Rights of Man and the Liberties of the World but Loose-Fish?" Similarly, as we have seen, on the international scene he objected to imposition of power by strong nations over weaker, even his own country—"What at last will Mexico be to the United States?" He pondered as well the anti-intellectualism and cultural decline which accompanied the obsession with materialism and deplored, too, the short-sighted xenophobia which made the masses vulnerable to demagogues, of whom there was no shortage in the mid-nineteenth century, as in almost every other era.

Nevertheless, Melville by no means lost his faith in democracy as an ideal. His thought was that instead of a facile, nationalistic conception of democracy based on the naïve faith of a pioneer spirit, America should develop a mature concept of democracy raised to a universal plane. The basis of this would be the re-creation of the spiritual energy of the individual living in a world of social justice and freedom. Although Melville did not deprecate the role of social reform through law in mitigating abuses, his writings reveal that he held fast to a deep belief that the acceptance of moral responsibility by the individual in his contacts with his fellow men and with Nature would form the matrix from which a noble society could evolve. Morality could not be legislated.

In the gam of the *Samuel Enderby* is reflected the good will toward the British Empire which Melville encouraged in *Mardi*. Nevertheless, Ahab's actions toward Captain Boomer and Dr. Bunger display not even a modicum of moral responsibility for working together to ameliorate the harsh conditions of human life in a precarious world, represented by the voyages of the whalers on the unpredictable ocean. It would appear that Melville thought that the United States could be blundering by not taking an attitude of cooperation with Britain, for in this world everyone needs friends, and who but Britain, Melville might ask, would be a true friend of the United States if serious trouble came?

Captain Boomer's attitude differs markedly from that shown by Captain Derick of the *Jungfrau*, the captain of the *Bouton de Rose*, and Ahab in that the Briton realizes that there is a problem which concerns all whaleships in those waters haunted by the White Whale; he knows that the wounds which Moby Dick can inflict are likely to be fatal and therefore should be avoided, and that there are values more important to whalemen than his pursuit.

The United States and Britain shared a common language, and Melville felt that this sharing formed a special relationship which precluded their being "foreigners" to each other, even aside from the geopolitical aspects of their affiliation. In Melville's day a distinct unity of purpose with Britain afforded a harbor of security for the United States as she grew to economic maturity under the protection of the British Navy, which guarded the sea lanes and protected American trade. Not only this, but there were strong cultural ties which spoke for the advantage of mutual cooperation. An education at Oxford or Cambridge gave even Americans an edge in the competitive world of the nineteenth century, boarding schools gave "finish" to the debutantes of wealthy families, and the educated middle classes looked to England as the arbiter of literature.[27] In England, too, there was much excitement to know about the strange new world coming into being in America—a stream of travelers came to take notes for books for the British reading public's edification.

Melville emphasized the mutual interests of the British and American whaling industries, but he also noted the "foibles" of each group. The British held to the notion of class superiority even in this enterprise: Ishmael good-humoredly notes that English whaleman thought of the Americans as "sea-peasants":

> Nor would difference of country make any very essential difference; that is, so long as both parties speak one language, as is the

[27]Melville, however, strongly urged writers to break away from this pattern, exhorting them in "Hawthorne and His Mosses," to break away from England's undue literary influence.

case with Americans and English. Though, to be sure, from the small number of English whalers, such meetings do not very often occur, and when they do occur there is too apt to be a sort of shyness between them; for your Englishman is rather reserved, and your Yankee, he does not fancy that sort of thing in anybody but himself. Besides, the English whalers sometimes affect a kind of metropolitan superiority over the American whalers; regarding the long, lean Nantucketer, with his nondescript provincialism, as a sort of sea-peasant. But where this superiority in the English whalemen does really consist, it would be hard to say, seeing that the Yankees in one day, collectively, kill more whales than all the English, collectively, in ten years. But this is a harmless little foible in the English whale-hunters, which the Nantucketer does not take much to heart, probably, because he knows that he has a few foibles himself.[28]

It was generally believed, rightly or wrongly, that the British, with their prestigious world empire, had a tolerant, enlightened, and self-assured attitude toward the world, an attitude similar to that displayed by Dr. Bunger and Captain Boomer. Evidently Melville found much to admire in this stance, although it does not necessarily follow that he considered it without defects. After all, Liverpool, the city where Melville had observed shocking social injustices, was in England; admirable as English foreign policy may have seemed, a factory system spawned by untrammeled capitalism had grown up there, too. Yet, characteristically, Melville was willing to believe that England of all countries was most likely to have the will to right the wrongs of a system which brought

---

[28]This passage points up one of the inconsistencies of Melville's thought regarding natural resources. Although at times he saw the danger to the globe in untrammeled exploitation, he also was so enthusiastic about America's future that at times he seemed to forget that America might go the way of other societies in the past if all his predictions came true.

so much misery to those who were unable to partake of the abundance their labor had made available to their country-men.[29] Melville would certainly have thought it logical, and ironic, for Karl Marx to have written his *Das Kapital* in the British Museum.[30] He would have been interested in Marx's analysis, but never would he have accepted the inevitability, much less the desirability, of class warfare.

Not one of the relationships described in these three gams contains indications of cooperation on the part of Ahab and his crew toward the other whalers, except in regard to their giving of oil to the ungrateful *Jungfrau*, but neither do they feel that they have any special obligation to cooperate at all.[31] Toward the complement of the French and German ships the men of the *Pequod* exhibit a nonchalant ethnocentrism, accompanied by some clumsy humor at the expense of the foreigners. This was especially noticeable in the case of the *Jungfrau* and the *Bouton de Rose*, for those on board were "more foreign" than the British on the *Samuel Enderby*: they spoke another "lingo." Naturally we are not expecting to see the sophistication of diplomats reflected in the actions of whalemen, but Melville evidently finds these attitudes characteristic among those in the general population whom he expected to be his readers.

---

[29] The chapter "Heads or Tails" contains an entertaining parable on this general subject.

[30] Marx's first edition of this work appeared in 1867.

[31] They did, however, feel that Abab should have assisted the *Rachel* in the search for the missing crewmen, but Captain Gardiner was not a "foreigner.".

We can hardly call Melville an internationalist in the modern sense of the word. Indeed, it would be nearer the truth to call him a nationalist, for he proudly shared the assumptions of his countrymen that America would someday fall heir to the political supremacy of the world, as he indicated in his essay, "Hawthorne and His Mosses." How Melville expected the United States to accomplish this in the world as it existed then without going to war is problematic, for historically that was the way nations gained domination. Melville would not choose this route for his country, but as for war, he had no illusions about its disappearance from the world scene, since he often admitted that conflict seemed to be an intrinsic part of man's nature. World peace would be more difficult to achieve than a mere political and military hegemony imposed by one nation on another, he thought, as he wrote in *Mardi*:

> The world's peaces are but truces. Long absent, at last the red comets have returned. And return they must though their periods be ages. And should the world endure till mountain melt into mountain, and all the isles form one tableland, yet it would but expand the old battle plain.

Unlike the majority of his compatriots, Melville could see that the problems of one nation closely affect the well-being of another, for he perceived how the destinies of people were inextricably bound together. Nowhere is this more evident than in the gam of the *Rachel*, which stresses the universality underlying the concept of human kinship. Nationalism, however, was rife in the nineteenth century, when the existence of competing national states was accepted as a normal basis for international relations, with personal diplomacy by an élite class one of the instruments by which wars were kept at a "reasonable" minimum and were waged for meaningful goals within that ideology.

What were these "meaningful goals"? In the nineteenth century wars were usually fought for expansion of territory on land or overseas: it is not likely that Melville would think this justification for risking the sufferings the war would bring. He would group the soldier with the factory worker and the plantation slave, for they, too, were slaves to machines—and had even less freedom than slaves, for they were "tools" flagrantly exploited (insidiously trained for killing) and were part of the machines which made war possible. Yet, unhappily, it was not difficult through propaganda to convince men such as those on the *Jeroboam* that they had a mission. Each war has its Gabriel who provides the slogans which incite citizens to go to war willingly (more or less) when the voice of reason is drowned out.[32] Melville had seen that phenomenon in the Mexican War: he was familiar with the slogan of "Manifest Destiny." This is just what he feared— that society would adopt the attitude that Heaven (or Fate) willed men to go to war.[33]

Nevertheless, many of his attitudes were ambivalent, some even seem naïve to us in the more realistic twentieth century. He reasoned that because American democracy was the hope of the world the United States was justified in seizing the lands of the Indians ("political pagans") who would eventually benefit from their civilizing alliance with the

---

[32]In *Mein Kampf* Adolf Hitler gives a chilling exposition of the use of propaganda. See Chapter VI.

[33]As the *Jeroboam*'s Gabriel used his "manifesto" as propaganda.

usurpers.[34] As for his practical stance on slavery, he did not want to risk shipwrecking the whole society to cure its ills: that would not necessarily effect the needed changes in individuals, and the dislocations could cause even greater suffering, he believed, as he hoped for a national agreement on a legal way to demolish the nefarious structure on which the Southern plantation system was constructed.

Although Melville held no brief for the purity of English industrialism or imperialism, as his comments in previous writings prove, it is not unlikely that he observed humanitarian trends in English political thought. He admired the action of the British in outlawing institutional slavery in their colonies and reproved his own country for not doing likewise. Later the British went as far as to say that they would like to see slavery abolished in the new territory of Texas, as well as in the established American South, a statement which alienated the powerful segments of the American population which had a stake in its continuance and which resented such "meddling" in American internal affairs.[35]

Melville saw slavery as a malignant cancer upon the body of American society. In 1851 the slavery question, though intensely troubling, could be looked upon by many Northerners in a somewhat abstract way, in contrast to the attitude of Southerners whose way of life was based upon it, socially

---

[34]Even so, he defended the Indians from historians' prejudices in a review of Parkman's *Oregon Trail* published in the *Literary World* on March 31, 1849.

[35]That British foreign policy was not wholly righteous is to be expected, since both economic and moral considerations had weight. Britain gave support to the Southern cause in the Civil War because her mills needed its cotton. Expediency allowed this, since slavery was legal in the United States. See Karcher.

and economically. But when after the Civil War it became apparent that there were no easy solutions to the problem of the integration of the freed slaves into the mainstream of American life, all areas of the country came to be deeply affected. Britain's surprise at the American refusal to recognize its own domestic dilemma might be seen as comparable to Captain Boomer's and Dr. Bunger's amazement at Ahab's refusal to recognize the folly of pursuing a dangerous course which would have dire consequences. Paralleling the American attitude in this regard was that of the captain of the *Bouton de Rose*, who could not perceive a serious problem on his ship even when it was under his own nose. Melville feared that the United States was fated to go through much suffering because of its stubborn espousal of slavery for so long. As it turned out, Ahab's dangerous course did mean death for him, and the issue of slavery brought about a devastating civil war for the United States. In both cases the innocent were caught up and destroyed in the maelstrom with the guilty.

A New Foundation for a New World

The three captains— Ahab, Derick, and the Frenchman— were intent upon their own goals; they were indifferent or unaware that a general mortal danger existed. Captain Boomer had suffered and he wished to spare others a similar suffering; Ahab had suffered, too, but he was not concerned with avoiding danger, neither was he solicitous about warning others. Captain Boomer assumed that a common awareness of danger should be a cohesive factor in society, a basis for mutual understanding, but Ahab peremptorily refused to accept this, obsessed as he was with his single-minded quest for self-assertion, and complacent as he was for the most part concerning his own ability to be master of his fate. The captain of the *Bouton de Rose* was naïve about the reality of his situation and unless he learned to confront the truth he would no doubt repeat his blunders.[36] As for Captain Derick, there was nothing to be expected from him but ingratitude and hostile rivalry.

Three Gams Provide the Answers Ahab Rejects

In the gams of the *Bachelor*, the *Rachel*, and the *Delight*, one can discern a similar theme under different circumstances—the communality of experience. Both happiness and grief can be shared, and should be shared, for these are the essence of the human condition. Ahab, in rejecting his ties to his own kind and denying the opportunity of that sharing to his crew, showed that human happiness and grief were all the same to him, as nothing compared to his own self-centered strivings.

Although Melville is convinced that moral responsibility on every level of human conduct is the necessary burden that must be taken up by each person, he is nevertheless ambivalent about the possibility that it will be achieved, for who can know the true nature of mankind? The lessons of *Ecclesiastes* and *Job* had found their way deep into his soul, and experience had dimmed the sheen of his optimism. At times he seemed to doubt the worth of his strenuous efforts to make

---

[36]Would Melville have thought the French had blundered in their political life which included a revolution, an empire under Napoleon (with disastrous wars), monarchy again, with Napoleon III on the throne by 1848?

himself understood and envied those who could enjoy simple-hearted pleasures:

> I have perceived in all cases that a man must eventually lower, or at least shift, his conceit of attainable felicity; not placing it anywhere in the intellect or the fancy, but in the wife, the heart, the bed, the table, the saddle, the fire-side, the country . . . . [37]

Only by accepting the common bond which holds all people within it and by finding in oneself compassion for each one who shares the common fate of humanity can the loneliness and alienation of the individual be assuaged, Melville implies. This compassion cannot be abstract, however. Even Ahab had words to express a generic compassion for mankind's struggles when he exclaimed: "By heaven, man, we are turned round and round in this world, like yonder windlass, and Fate is the handspike." Starbuck almost believed that his captain's heart could be touched. But his compassion was sterile.

Within the individual, within domestic society, and in relations with other peoples of the world, Melville sought to find a unity of destiny which bound all spheres of human activity into a totality, one to be ignored only at humanity's peril. The omnipresent cruelty, violence, greed, poverty, and exploitation were to be deplored; to fathom their causes and attempt to find solutions was the moral responsibility of all. This was Melville's conviction, one to which he devoted his pen, even when his message was disdained.

---

[37] In "A Squeeze of the Hand." Here we are safe in assuming that it is Melville who is speaking, since Ishmael never mentions a wife or home.

13

Epilogue

The gams of the *Pequod* could conceivably have been meetings in actual time and space with actual men involved. If
Ahab had allowed it, his lonely crew could have spun yarns
and sung ditties during gams with their fellows on the
whaleships they encountered. Instead of that, their gams are
abortive and permeated with sadness. In the solitary sinking
of the *Pequod* Melville found a symbol which conveys the
reality of a man's descent into a spiritual void when he will-
fully exploits or disdains every human relationship, even to
using his power to shape others' lives to suit his own purpose. This, Melville tells us, is the danger which America was
courting: that she should lose sight of the dignity and glory of
the individual, around whom her ideals ostensibly clustered.

The quest which is the prevailing theme of *Moby–Dick*
will end on a note of hope. After the futile chase for Moby
Dick ends in disaster for all but Ishmael, Melville has the
Rachel return, still searching for her missing "children."[1] With

---

[1] References to the Biblical Rachel are found in *Jeremiah* 31:15 and *Matthew*
2:18—"A voice is heard in Ramah, mourning and great weeping, Rachel
weeping for her children, and refusing to be comforted, because her children are

her return Melville makes the Biblical implications of his message explicit. The refusal of Captain Gardiner to give up the search for his son and his other lost crewmen was the cause of Ishmael's rescue. The decision of one individual, the captain, saved the life of another.

Ishmael survives the ordeal of loneliness, is saved by the ship which symbolizes an intense faith in the value of life, one, too, that is epitomized by the image of the mother, civilization's enduring symbol for unselfish love.

The symbol of Nantucket, or wherever home may be, shines like a star in the imagination of the men who have families there waiting for their eventual return. There wait three mothers who endure the long vigil for the return of the *Pequod* in vain: Ahab's wife, Starbuck's wife, and Flask's mother. Although *Moby-Dick* has been generally seen as a book devoted to masculine exploits and themes, a consistent underlying *motif* is that of the woman, whose spirit and faith form the stability of life and give meaning to the enterprise in which the men are engaged—if they are fortunate enough to have found the woman to create this meaning. Starbuck's characterization is the mirror, the "magic glass" of this *motif*: his yearning for the qualities of life represented by the woman and child is the motivation for his constraint toward Ahab and his entreaties to him to relinquish the doomed quest. Starbuck's fate is truly a tragic one, for he was caught in a dilemma from which there was no escape.

no more." These passages, however, refer to a symbolic Biblical Rachel.

Ironically, no one is waiting for Ishmael. Ishmael, the enigma, is saved to resume his circumnavigation—to begin his voyages again, a wanderer on that sea which is, in Melville's words, "the image of the ungraspable phantoms of life, and this is the key to it all."

The lessons suggested by the gams lead us back to the traditional moral teachings, whose precepts were transmuted into some of Melville's own conclusions on possible solutions to modern dilemmas. He was not sure that a way ever could be found which would lead human beings unfalteringly to the happiness they sought. They must accept the existence of evil along with any good they might receive from an inscrutable universe. Along with this resignation (reminiscent of Father Mapple) must come faith in the eventual liberation from torment. Melville has Vivenza give this answer in *Mardi*, responding to the question, "Say thou, in what wise shall [suffering] be relieved?":

> "The future is all hieroglyphics. Who may read? But methinks the great laggard Time must now march up apace and somehow befriend these thralls. It cannot be that misery is perpetually entailed."

In the midst of this misery, however, love is possible, as the return of the *Rachel* suggests. Melville does not try to convince us that the transformation of the human spirit through that love will ever be easy, however. We will find that we must supply the faith; we must supply the effort, as he did. But the epilogue to *Clarel*, his last work, echoes the theme of the epilogue to his greatest work, *Moby-Dick*. In both he expresses his conviction that it is on a personal, private level, in the individual heart, that this progress may be truly achieved. Clarel is exhorted to keep high his faith in the reality of spiritual values in human existence, to resist forever the temptation to give credence to a materialist dogma, for the evidence of the senses does not represent the whole truth of the universe. It might be, as Starbuck reflects, that "faith must oust facts":

Then keep thy heart, though yet but ill resigned—
Clarel, thy heart, the issues there but mind;
That like the crocus budding through the snow—
That like a swimmer rising from the deep—
That like a burning secret which doth go
Even from the bosom that would hoard and keep;
Emerge thou mayst from the last whelming sea,
And prove that death but routs life into victory.

And so the voyage ends and *Moby-Dick* comes to a close:

". . . A sail drew near, near, and picked me up at last. It was the devious-cruising Rachel, that in her retracing search after her missing children, only found another orphan."

Selected Bibliography

Herman Melville's Works

"The Tartarus of Maids," in *American Issues: The Social Record,* edited by Willard Thorp. Chicago: J. B. Lippincott Company, 1944.

Clarel: A Poem and Pilgrimage in the Holy Land. Edited by Walter E. Bezanson. New York: Hendricks House, 1960.

"Hawthorne and His Mosses," in *American Literary Essays,* edited by Lewis Leary. New York: Thomas Y. Crowell, 1960.

Mardi. Edited by Harrison Hayford, Hershel Parker, and G. Thomas Tanselle. Evanston and Chicago: Northwestern University Press and Newberry Library, 1970.

Moby-Dick or, *The Whale.* Edited by Charles Feidelson, Jr. Indianapolis: The Bobbs-Merrill Company, 1964.

Redburn: His First Voyage.. Edited by Harrison Hayford, Hershel Parker, and G. Thomas Tanselle. Evanston and Chicago: Northwestern University Press and Newberry Library, 1969.

Secondary Works

Ahearn, Edward J. *Marx and Modern Fiction.* New Haven: Yale University Press, 1989.

Arvin, Newton. "Melville and the Gothic Novel," in *American Pantheon.* New York: Delacorte Press, 1966.

Camus, Albert. "Herman Melville," in *Les Écrivains célèbres,* Vol. 3. Paris: Lucien Mazenod, 1953.

Capra, Fritjof. *The Turning Point: Science, Society, and the Rising Cullture.* New York: Simon and Schuster, 1982..

Eby, E. H. *Herman Melville's* "Tartarus of Maids," *Modern Language Quarterly,* I (March, 1940), 95-100.

Grejda, Edward S. *The Common Continent of Man: Racial Equality in the Writings of Herman Melville.* Port Washington, New York: Kennikat Press, 1974.

Grenberg, Bruce L. *Some Other Worlds to Find: Quest and Negation in the Works of Herman Melville.* Urbana: University of Illinois Press, 1989.

Handlin, Oscar. *Chance or Destiny: Turning Points in American History.* Boston: Little, Brown, 1955.

Hitler, Adolf. *Mein Kampf.* Translated by Ralph Manheim. Boston: Houghton Mifflin Company, 1943.

Hoffman, Stanley. *The State of War. Essays on the Theory and Practice of International Politics.* New York: Frederick A. Praeger, 1965.

Hofstader, Richard. *Social Darwinism in American Thought, 1860-1915* Philadelphia: University of Philadelphia Press, 1945.

Karcher, Carolyn L. *Shadow over the Promised Land: Slavery, Race, and Violence in Melville's America.* Baton Rouge: Louisiana State University, 1980.

Lucid, Robert F. "The Influence of *Two Years before the Mast* on Herman Melville," *American Literature,* XXXI (November, 1959), 243-56.

Marcell, David. *Progress and Pragmatism: James, Dewey, Beard, and the American Idea of Progress.* Westport, Connecticut: Greenwood Press, 1974.

Marx, Leo. *The Machine in the Garden: Technology and the Pastoral Ideal in America.* New York: Oxford University Press, 1964.

Matthiessen., F. O. *American Renaissance: Art and Expression in the Age of Emerson and Whitman.* London: Oxford University Press, 1966.

Mayhew, Henry. *London Labour and the London Poor.* London: Griffin, Bohn, and Company, 1861.

Mayoux, Jean-Jacques. *Melville.* Translated by John Ashbery. New York: Grove Press, 1960.

Parker, Hershel, and Harrison Hayford, eds. *Moby-Dick as Doubloon: Essays and Extracts (1851-1970).* New York: W. W. Norton, 1970.

Sealts, Merton M. *Melville's Reading.* Columbia: University of South Carolina Press, 1988.

Sewall, Richard B. *The Vision of Tragedy: Tragic Themes in Literature from the Book of Job to O'Neill and Miller.* New edition, enlarged. New York: Paragon House, 1990.

Sherrill, Rowland A. *The Prophetic Melville.* Athens: University of Georgia Press, 1979.

Smith, Huston, ed. *The Search for America.* Englewood Cliffs, New Jersey: Prentice Hall, 1959.

Spiller, Robert E. *et al.,* eds. *Literary History of the United States.* Third edition, revised. New York: The Macmillan Company, 1963.

Sullivan, J. W. N. "Herman Melville," *London Times Literary Supplement,* 1123 (July 26, 1923), 493-94.

Taylor, A. J. P. *Bismarck: The Man and the Statesman.* New York: Alfred A. Knopf, 1955.

Thorp, Willard. *Herman Melville: Representative Selections.* New York: American Book Company, 1938.

Wright, Nathalia. *Melville's Use of the Bible.* New York: Octagon Books, 1969.

Index

Index

F

factory system, 107, 112, 120, 131
false prophets, 120
family, 6, 79, 80, 84, 95, 100
fanaticism, 119, 121
fast fish, 59, 124
Fate, 32, 33, 45, 49, 77, 79, 80, 81, 82, 89,94, 138
Father Mapple, 9, 89, 93
Feidelson, Charles, Jr., 2
fishes, 20, 26, 80
Flask, 24, 48, 52, 75, 84
France, 137
Frenchmen, 55, 58
Freud, Sigmund, 31, 44, 52
frontier life, 118

G

"Gabriel," 36, 42, 44, 89, 119, 123
gam, definition of, 15
gamming, 16
gams as mirrors, 6, 111
gams as messages, 14
Germany, 49, 124, 125
goals of society, 104, 105, 106, 108, 120, 134
Golden Inn, 28, 117
gospel of wealth, 112
government, 116
greed, 101, 112, 129

H

harpoon, Ahab's, 73, 92
Hawthorne, Nathaniel, 105, 133
Hitler, Adolf, 120, 125, 134n
hospitality, 67, 74
human nature, 22, 33, 42, 44, 51, 52, 53, 69, , 125
human relationships, xi, 9, 12, 25, 31, 33, 45, 51, 54, 57, 62, 76, 112, 126, 137, 138
humanitarianism, 131
humor, 31, 47, 50, 56, 59

I

Indians, North American, 21
individual, 34, 44, 86, 138, 141
industrialization, 99, 104, 107, 108, 113, 126, 127,131
Inquisition, 118
international relations, 123, 124, 128, 130, 132,133 , 136
irrationality, 42, 90, 116
Ishmael, 10, 28, 29, 30, 32, 41,67,86, 95, 113, 119, 141, 142,

J

Japanese Sea, 71
Jeroboam, 35, 119, 121
Jungfrau, 47, 123, 125

K

kinship, 6, 12, 24, 95

L

law, 42, 44, 111, 116, 117, 124, 128
leaders, 42, 89, 122
legalism, 42, 58, 60
letters, 25, 39
Lima (Peru), 29, 117
Liverpool (England), 100
loose fish, 58, 124, 127
loyalty, 76

M

machine age, 13, 107
madness, 22, 23, 32, 34, 36, 76, 89, 106, 121
"magic glass," xiii, 80, 140
mail on whalers, 25, 39
Mardi, 76, 104, 129, 133, 141
Marx, Karl, 37n
materialism, 14, 107, 128
meaning, 5, 6, 22, 44, 88, 93
Melville, Herman
  ambiguity, 134, 135, 137
  as mutineer, 24, 41